The Royal Baccarat Scandal

A play

Royce Ryton

Based on the book by
Michael Havers and Edward Grayson

Samuel French – London
New York – Sydney – Toronto – Hollywood

© 1990 BY ROYCE RYTON

1. *This play is fully protected under the Copyright Laws of the British Commonwealth of Nations, the United States of America and all countries of the Berne and Universal Copyright Conventions.*

2. *All rights, including Stage, Motion Picture, Radio, Television, Public Reading and Translation into Foreign Languages, are strictly reserved.*

---

3. **No part of this publication may lawfully be reproduced in ANY form or by any means—photocopying, typescript, recording (including video-recording), manuscript, electronic, mechanical, or otherwise—or be transmitted or stored in a retrieval system, without prior permission.**

---

4. Rights of Performance by Amateurs are controlled by SAMUEL FRENCH LTD, 52 FITZROY STREET, LONDON W1P 6JR, and they, or their authorized agents, issue licences to amateurs on payment of a fee. **It is an infringement of the Copyright to give any performance or public reading of the play before the fee has been paid and the licence issued.**

5. Licences are issued subject to the understanding that it shall be made clear in all advertising matter that the audience will witness an amateur performance; that the names of the authors of the plays shall be included on all announcements and on all programmes; and that the integrity of the author's work will be preserved.

    The Royalty Fee indicated below is subject to contract and subject to variation at the sole discretion of Samuel French Ltd.

    > Basic fee for each and every
    > performance by amateurs   Code M
    > in the British Isles

    In Theatres or Halls seating Six Hundred or more the fee will be subject to negotiation.

    In Territories Overseas the fee quoted above may not apply. A fee will be quoted on application to our local authorized agent, or if there is no such agent, on application to Samuel French Ltd, London.

6. The Professional Rights in this play are controlled by MICHAEL IMISON PLAYWRIGHTS LTD, 28 Almeida Street, London N1 1TD.

The publication of this play does not imply that it is necessarily available for performance by amateurs or professionals, either in the British Isles or Overseas. Amateurs and professionals considering a production are strongly advised in their own interests to apply to the appropriate agents for consent before starting rehearsals or booking a theatre or hall.

ISBN 0 573 11374 2

THE ROYAL BACCARAT SCANDAL

First presented at the Chichester *festival* Theatre and subsequently by Duncan C Weldon and Jerome Minskoff for Triumph Theatre Productions Ltd at the Theatre Royal, Haymarket, London, on 21st February 1989, with the following cast

Sir William Gordon Cumming	Keith Michell
Mrs Gibbs, his daughter	Jackie Smith-Wood
HRH the Prince of Wales	Rowland Davies
General Williams, his ADC	John McCallum
Ethel Lycett Green	Fiona Fullerton
Mr Lycett Green	Gary Bond
Mrs Wilson	Jeannette Sterke
Stanley Wilson, her son	Laurence Kennedy
Mrs Williams, the General's wife	Marianne Morley
Mr Levett, a young officer	Paul M. Meston
Sir Edward Clarke QC	Gerald Harper
Sir Charles Russell QC	Philip Stone
The French Chef	Christopher Leaver
Jarvis, Sir William's batman	Michael Fleming
Housekeeper	Jacqueline Lacey
The Prince's Mistress	Andrea Wray
Miss Naylor	Harriet Benson
Court Officials	Simon Packham
	Sean Patterson
	Stanley Page

Directed by Val May
Designed by Tim Goodchild

The play begins in 1922 in Sir William Gordon Cumming's country house in Scotland. Subsequently most of the action takes place between 1890 and 1891 in various locations, including the Lycett Greens' house in London, the Wilsons' house at Tranby Croft and the Lord Chief Justice's Court.

CHARACTERS

Sir William Gordon Cumming
Mrs Gibbs, his daughter
General Williams, ADC to the Prince
HRH The Prince of Wales
Ethel Lycett Green
Mr Lycett Green
Mrs Wilson
Stanley Wilson, her son
Mrs Williams, the General's wife
Mr Levett, a young officer
Sir Edward Clarke QC
Sir Charles Russell QC
Jarvis, Sir William's batman
French Chef
Court Officials, Footmen, Ladies, Maids etc.

THE SET

The period is 1890, apart from the opening and closing moments which take place in 1922. The set is all purpose, but is basically a nineteenth-century country house in Scotland. Most of the action takes place on the main stage, which can be anything and anywhere we wish it to be—a drawing room, a park in London, a barrister's rooms, a Court Room. Behind is a built-up area with wide steps in the centre and a large pillar. There is a raised balcony, left, and a higher balcony, right, under which is a door. There is a suggestion here and there of oak panelling, hunting trophies and regimental souvenirs—but this area too can be anything we wish it to be—the Prince of Wales' dressing room, a hall, a conservatory. There are steps up to it from behind and entrances from either side. The main item of furniture is a large but easily movable chair on the main stage—Sir William's chair. Its usual position is near the centre down stage. There is very little other furniture in this area except a comfortable tapestry stool for Mrs Gibbs, two tables up stage and a few chairs.

The character Mrs Gibbs is not only Sir William's daughter, she is also the play's narrator as well. Only Sir William and the audience see her, NONE of the other characters in the play do so.

The lighting is important and at certain times will be highly selective. Sound will often be used to evoke atmosphere.

ACT I

The play begins with Sir William alone on the stage

After a moment Mrs Gibbs enters

Mrs Gibbs Well, they've gone. At last. I thought some of them would never leave. But the flowers were lovely, weren't they?

She gets no reply from her father and evidently doesn't expect one. She tidies up the remains of the refreshments

A wake always seems to me to be a very curious form of entertainment. I had no idea Mother was so popular with all the villagers and tenants . . . I mean hundreds were at the church and I don't know how many came back here.

Sir William No one was there at all. No one, that matters.

Mrs Gibbs Did you expect anything different?

Sir William No.

Mrs Gibbs You haven't touched the claret cup. I made it myself.

Sir William You never took your eyes off me in church.

Mrs Gibbs Didn't I, Father? I'm sorry. I was wondering what you were thinking.

Sir William I shouldn't let that concern you.

Mrs Gibbs No . . . Well . . . I'll tell you what I was thinking in church, Father. That I am thirty years old, have had two children and am about to be divorced, and that I cannot recall a single intimate conversation with you in all that time. Why do we never talk?

Sir William listens impassively

Mrs Gibbs turns to the audience

I was twenty before I fully understood how very peculiar our lives were. Here I was in nineteen-twelve, the daughter of a baronet living in Scotland with a rich American mother and we knew nobody. The balls and house parties I should have gone to, I never went to. The friends I should have had I didn't have. I once went on a weekend with my husband, so naturally I was introduced as Mrs Gibbs. All the others knew each other, had been brought up together. I didn't know anyone. Somehow the conversation turned to names and I was asked what my maiden name was. In all innocence I said Gordon Cumming and I might have dropped a bomb. The dinner table was silent and everyone stared at me as if I had some dreadful sickness. (*She turns back to Sir William*) What happened, Father?

2   The Royal Baccarat Scandal

He is still silent

Surely, now Mother is dead, we can at least talk about it?

Pause

Sir William I was the victim of a young man's insane desire for revenge, we all were.

Mrs Gibbs (*to the audience*) For a moment I thought that was all he was going to say. And then, to my amazement ...

Sir William Do you know anything about my life at all?

Mrs Gibbs A little. Oh, I knew it was absolutely fatal to talk about the past either with you or with Mother—

Sir William (*tightly*) It was never discussed. With anyone.

Mrs Gibbs So I looked you up in *Who's Who*.

Sir William Good move. (*He sits in his chair*) You'd better pour me some of that claret cup of yours.

Mrs Gibbs I was most impressed. And even more puzzled. You'd had such a splendid career. Colonel in the Scots Guards. Zulu War. Gordon Relief Expedition. Big-game hunting in India. It was like reading about a stranger.

Sir William Do you know that stalking a tiger on foot is the most dangerous sport in the world? That's why I loved it. I didn't just want to kill. I wanted to risk my own neck too. There is no fun in anything without a risk ...

Mrs Gibbs You seem to have done everything, been everywhere.

Sir William Naturally. I was a member of the Prince of Wales's set. You can have no idea what that meant. It opened all doors for one. There wasn't an important house party to which I wasn't invited. There wasn't a scrap of gossip that I didn't share.

Mrs Gibbs Gossip?

Sir William About the second most dangerous sport.

Mrs Gibbs What was that?

Sir William Adultery. At all the dinner parties, once the ladies had gone, the favourite topic over the port was who was sleeping with whom. (*He laughs*) It was a sort of secret Society game—chasing other men's wives. We did it because it was fun to outwit the husbands. And we did it because it was dangerous. Discovery meant instant disgrace.

Mrs Gibbs So a scandal was not part of the fun?

Sir William Only when it happened to somebody else. And certainly not if the Prince was involved.

General Williams appears from the background. He is a man of about sixty, the Prince's ADC. He is in a very convivial mood, drinking brandy, smoking a cigar, laughing. He is accompanied by two Young Men. All are in evening dress

General Williams (*laughing*) I could tell you stories about HRH that would make your hair stand on end. I don't know how he gets away with it.

Sir William Damned if I do either.

Act I 3

They all roar with laughter

What would you say was his closest shave?

General Williams I'd say the Churchill business. The Prince had gone to stay with the Marlboroughs at Blenheim.

Sir William The General in his cups could be very indiscreet.

General Williams And Randolph was there with his latest filly—you know the Walters girl.

Sir William (*to the Young Men*) Known as "Skittles" because everybody played with her.

General Williams Mind you she made it an easy game to play.

Sir William The Prince was bowled over by her at once wasn't he?

General Williams Well of course, and at the very first opportunity he ... Oh, but my lips are sealed, I mustn't say another word.

Sir William Wouldn't do for his ADC. HRH made a beeline for her bedroom.

General Williams And hopped into bed. And there he was *in flagrante delicto*——

Young Man In flagrante de what?

Sir William Hard at it.

General Williams When Randolph came in. The Prince leapt out of bed——

Sir William Stark naked I believe.

General Williams Absolutely stitchless.

Sir William Randolph fell into a rage——

General Williams And chased the Prince round the room and down the corridor—straight into the arms of the Duchess.

All laugh

Sir William
General Williams } (*together*) And that was the end of Randolph.

All laugh

Sir William (*chuckling*) The Prince cut him dead until he died.

They all roar with laughter

General Williams Nothing will stop HRH, you know. He's probably hard at it now. My lips are sealed. My lips are sealed.

The light fades on them and comes up on another side of the stage. The Prince of Wales is dressing. An attractive Girl in a negligée is handing him his shirt and cravat, etc. The Prince, later Edward VII, was then fifty years old, undeniably portly in figure. He holds himself well. When fully dressed in his beautifully cut clothes, he is an impressive-looking man. He has great dignity and charm

Prince What you've got to understand, my dear, is that everyone gossips about me. I sometimes think that is what a Prince of Wales is for. But it doesn't matter, my dear, as long as it doesn't get into the papers. What

4   The Royal Baccarat Scandal

puzzles my mother and all the radicals is that despite my wicked ways, I am very popular with the working class because I do what they all want to do. They would like to have race horses, they would like to go to Paris without their wives. They would like to have my success with women. They would like to be rich, have a title and travel round Europe, and the reason they don't hate me for being able to do it when they can't is because I so obviously enjoy it all. Appearances are everything, you see. They allow people to believe that we are perfect. Only we aren't are we? (*He kisses her*) So we must settle for the next best thing—we must never be found out. Gossip is quite another matter. It goes on in Society, which is safe. I positively encourage it because everyone enjoys it so much and nobody really believes it. What my detractors don't understand is that actually I am rather clever. They won't find it out until I'm King and then I shall astonish them. My buttonhole, my dear. Thank you. Remember me to your husband. He's such an understanding man.

The lighting fades on them and comes up on Sir William and Mrs Gibbs

Sir William It was a chance meeting that began it all. In Hyde Park. It's quite thirty years or so since I've been there. I'm told it's all changed. But then one met one's friends there. People in Society—and—oh yes—even the Prince of Wales.

The Lights cross-fade

Prince Ah, Gordon Cumming.

Sir William bows respectfully

Sir William Your Royal Highness.
Prince The very person.
Sir William Sir?
Prince Doing anything for the Doncaster races?
Sir William Not at the moment, sir.
Prince My horse is running in the St Leger and my usual hosts are away, so I'm staying with the Wilsons at Tranby Croft. Do you know them?
Sir William The Wilsons?
Prince Ship-builder fellow. Very well heeled.
Sir William Ah yes. From Hull, I believe.
Prince That's the chap. Charming wife and family. Pretty daughter. Married that Lycett Green fellow.
Sir William Yes, indeed.
Prince I'll get them to invite you. They're a man short, they tell me.

He begins to move off with Sir William

The Prince of Wales exits

The Lights fade to a spot on Sir William

Sir William Seldom can an invitation have had such disastrous results. That innocent encounter in Hyde Park changed all our lives. Had the Prince gone to any other house there would have been no scandal. But now

Act I   5

everyone was racing excitedly towards the crisis of their lives. None more so than our hostess, Mrs Wilson, whose chance to break into Society had miraculously arrived. In a frenzy of last-minute preparations she called on her daughter in London.

Sir William exits

The Lights come up

> *Mrs Wilson hurries on, dressed in travelling clothes, followed by her daughter, Ethel Lycett Green*

Mrs Wilson The Prince is frightfully particular about his food, so I've engaged this brilliant French chef.

Stanley Wilson enters

Stanley Mother, the cab has arrived.
Mrs Wilson He's terribly temperamental and demanding. But I don't care.
Ethel Darling, you'll miss your train.
Stanley And if we miss it, there's not another one until after lunch.
Mrs Wilson Every meal must be a triumph, especially now Lady Brooke can't come. Can you imagine the shock when she cancelled—she of all people.
Ethel We can easily manage without Lady Brooke, Mother.
Stanley My charming sister only has to make eyes at the Prince and he'll forget all about his mistress.
Mrs Wilson Friend, Stanley. We don't say "mistress". Special friend. And I was absolutely relying on her to keep him amused and happy.
Ethel Don't worry, Mother. I can look after him perfectly well.
Mrs Wilson It's no use telling me not to worry. I am worrying. About everything. The flowers, the decorations—have they finished the triumphal arch yet?
Stanley Long ago. And the marquee is up on the lawn and the cab is waiting but the train won't.
Mrs Wilson If only your father would help.
Ethel At least he's meeting the Prince at the station.
Mrs Wilson What?
Stanley You know, the reception party on the platform.
Ethel With the Lord Lieutenant and the Yorkshire Volunteers lined up behind.
Mrs Wilson Yes, but if we're all at the station——
Stanley We're not.
Mrs Wilson Who on earth receives him at the house?
Ethel
Stanley } *(in chorus)* You do, Mother!
Mrs Wilson Do I? *(Shattered)* Oh my goodness, so I do!

Ethel can no longer restrain her laughter

Stanley That is if we ever get to Tranby Croft, which I very much doubt. And if we don't go now, we won't.

6   The Royal Baccarat Scandal

He starts to bundle Mrs Wilson out, but she turns back to her daughter

Stanley exits

Mrs Wilson Oh, darling, I almost forgot to tell you. We've got our extra
man.
Ethel (*still laughing*) Oh, who?
Mrs Wilson Sir William Gordon Cumming.
Stanley (*off*) Mother—for heaven's sake.
Mrs Wilson Yes, yes!

Mrs Wilson exits

Ethel's laughter dies, and she freezes in shock

*Off stage, we hear exclamations and greetings with Stanley's voice rising
impatiently*

Stanley (*off*) Oh hullo, we can't stop.
Lycett Green (*off*) Hullo.
Mrs Wilson (*off*) Lady Brooke's uncle has died, you see, so——
Stanley (*off*) Come *on*! Mother!

Lycett Green enters, smiling

Lycett Green Your mother does amuse me. Stanley virtually had to push
her out of the house. What train are we catching—the three-thirty—well,
we've got plenty of time. (*He notices his wife's silence*) What's the matter?
Ethel We can't go.
Lycett Green I beg your pardon?
Ethel We can't go to Tranby Croft. Not possibly.
Lycett Green Why on earth not?
Ethel Lady Brooke has cancelled.
Lycett Green Well?
Ethel Don't you see? I shall have to look after the Prince myself.
Lycett Green What of it? You're not a debutante going to her first party.
You've met the Prince several times before.
Ethel Yes, but . . .
Lycett Green In fact, last time I seem to remember you had quite a little
flirtation with him. So what's so different now?
Ethel Everything. Lady Brooke would have been beside him the whole
time, and now it will have to be me. I shall be lunching with him, driving
with him, dining with him, and I'm terrified.
Lycett Green Oh, really!
Ethel You know what the Prince is like. If the slightest thing goes wrong he
flies into a tantrum. Look at Lady Fitton. All she did was fall over her
train in front of him, and he banished her from Society!
Lycett Green Well he's not going to banish you. So I suggest you go
upstairs and pack.
Ethel Can't we say I'm ill?
Lycett Green No, we cannot.

Act I

Ethel I feel dreadful.

Lycett Green What is wrong with you?

Ethel I'm sick with nerves.

Lycett Green I refuse to pander to this nonsense. Please go and see to the luggage. We can't possibly insult the Prince by cancelling at the last moment.

Ethel Lady Brooke just has.

Lycett Green Lady Brooke has had a death in the family.

Ethel Couldn't you have one in yours?

Lycett Green I think you've gone off your head. Kindly stop this or I shall lose my temper. Half the country would give their right hand to spend the weekend with the Prince of Wales. It's the chance of a lifetime to get into his set, and I don't intend to let you ruin it.

Ethel Why are you so desperate to get into his set?

Lycett Green To get on in this world one has to know the right people.

Ethel We know hundreds of people. Father is one of the most successful men in the country.

Lycett Green Yes, in shipping, which is trade. My father is an MP, but he is also, alas, in trade. And people won't let us forget it. I can't get into the best clubs and we aren't invited to the best parties. I'm even lucky to be Master of the local Hunt.

Ethel (*near to tears*) Why do you always have to believe what a few snobs say? It's madness.

Lycett Green Is it madness to want the best future for our children? The Prince's visit could change everything for us. Without Lady Brooke there, you will have the perfect opportunity to cultivate him. To amuse him, to please him, to be altogether charming. And if he likes you we might even get an invitation to Sandringham.

Ethel And what if he doesn't like me?

Lycett Green Oh, he will. I'd count on it, my dear, with your many accomplishments. Why, you even play baccarat rather well.

Ethel Baccarat! What has that got to do with anything?

Lycett Green The Prince insists on playing it wherever he goes. He's obsessed by the game. And you've had lessons. You'll be able to impress him with your play and that will be a great point in our favour.

Ethel (*near to tears*) How can I play baccarat when my hands are shaking so much I won't be able to hold the cards. Please! Please don't make me go.

Lycett Green Why are you lying to me?

Ethel What?

Lycett Green Pretending to be ill. There's something else behind this, isn't there?

Ethel No! I am ill. I tell you, I'm ill.

Lycett Green I don't care if you are dying.

Ethel I may be pregnant.

Lycett Green (*furiously*) Nonsense! I don't think I've ever heard anything so selfish and hysterical in all my life.

Lycett Green storms off

8 The Royal Baccarat Scandal

Ethel (*following him, and shouting after him*) If I'm selfish, you are inconsiderate and unkind. I won't go! You can't make me go!

She is swallowed up in darkness

Sir William is spotlit on the right balcony

Sir William Baccarat ...

There is an echo of strange music, with the sound of clicking counters and distant voices murmuring the jargon of the game

Do you know anything about baccarat, my dear?

Mrs Gibbs No.

Sir William It was the latest craze. Everyone played it. I'm talking about eighteen-ninety. It swept Society very much as I believe mah-jong has today. The great difference being that bacarrat was technically illegal because it was a game of chance and not of skill. Be that as it may, very few people paid much attention, least of all the Prince, who always travelled with his own baccarat counters embossed with his Feathers in gold.

Mrs Gibbs And you went with him to Tranby Croft?

Sir William Of course. The excitement of joining the Royal train was tremendous. I loved it all—the pomp he delighted in like a child in a show—and above all, the knowledge that one was a favoured guest. It made one acutely—proud. Of course playing host to him was another matter, and fraught with peril.

The Lights go up on the main stage

The stage is suddenly alive with a flurry of activity. Parlour-maids hurry across with vases of flowers and fresh linens; Footmen carry trays of glasses and champagne buckets; and Mrs Wilson is in the middle of it all

Mrs Wilson (*to the Parlour-maids*) Roses and carnations in the blue bedroom, freesias and gardenias in the pink. (*To a passing Footman*) Please be careful with that, it belongs to Mr Wilson. (*To another Footman*) And for goodness' sake make sure the champagne is properly chilled!

The French Chef enters

Chef Madame, I must 'ave two extra 'ands in the kitchen—otherwise it is impossible.

Mrs Wilson Engage them, engage them. Anything you want. Are you quite sure you've remembered what the Prince has for breakfast?

Chef How could I forget? Kidney, liver, bacon, eggs, sausages, steak, coffee, champagne, porridge, cream, fruit, kedgeree. Does 'is Royal Highness eat it all?

Mrs Wilson All. And at eleven o'clock?

Chef Champagne, smoked salmon, caviar.

Sir William (*to Mrs Gibbs*) You see, the Prince could not last an hour without a four-course meal.

Chef It will probably kill us, but don't worry, madame.

Act I

Mrs Wilson If anyone else tells me not to worry, I shall scream.

The Lights go down on the main stage and crossfade to Mrs Gibbs and Sir William

Mrs Gibbs So the Wilsons were obviously *nouveaux riches.*
Sir William Undoubtedly. But the Prince never minded the *nouveaux riches* as long as they were *riche* enough. So it was all a touch too lavish but excellent nevertheless.
Mrs Gibbs Did you play baccarat on the first evening?
Sir William No, the Prince retired early. At the races the next day they cheered him when he arrived, cheered him when his horse won, cheered him when he left. And all the time he beamed and smiled and waved. The drive back to Tranby Croft was almost like a state procession. Mrs Wilson was beside herself with excitement. I thought she was going to go off her head. I dressed for dinner without a care in the world. I had no premonition, no sense of foreboding. Indeed, I had never looked forward to a brighter future.
Mrs Gibbs What did you hope lay ahead?
Sir William A peerage or a governorship at least. I had the world at my feet. I went down to dinner proud to be present at the Prince's special request. The meal was excellent, and after port and cigars we joined the ladies in the music room where Ethel Lycett Green sang to us . . .

The spot goes out on Sir William and the Lights come up on the main stage

The sound of Ethel's voice has crept in, and we hear the end of the song and enthusiastic applause

Sir William is by now seated in his chair, with Mrs Gibbs nearby. He must have both a commanding view of the stage and of the audience

The entire house party now enters onto the centre balcony, with the exception of Lycett Green. All are in full evening dress, the women sparkling in their finest jewellery. Most of the men are smoking cigars

Prince That was delightful, Mrs Wilson. I almost think I've eaten too much!
Mrs Wilson (*thrilled*) Oh sir!
Prince And your daughter sang charmingly. I'll wager she could have taken it up professionally.
Mrs Wilson She's had lessons from Jean de Reszke.
Prince Really? He has sung for us at Sandringham.

General and Mrs Williams draw near. Mrs Williams, aged about fifty or so is usually agitated about something or other, either with excitement or terror

General Williams My wife was saying what a splendid dinner it was, Mrs Wilson.
Mrs Williams Absolutely delicious!
Prince No one should entertain at all unless they can do it properly. Mrs Wilson, I shall call again!

Laughter

10 The Royal Baccarat Scandal

You have arranged my little visit to perfection.

Mrs Wilson You are most kind, sir.

The Prince smiles graciously and moves away to talk to others

Prince Ah! Williams! A word with you.

Mrs Wilson crosses to her son

Mrs Wilson (*glowing*) Did you hear that? His Royal Highness is pleased!

Stanley So he should be. Thank God his horse won this afternoon.

Mrs Wilson Just so long as he doesn't want to play cards. You know how Papa disapproves of baccarat.

Prince (*pricking up his ears*) Baccarat! Did I hear you suggest a game, Mrs Wilson? What an excellent idea! Why don't you lead the way to the card room?

Mrs Wilson (*stunned*) Card room. Oh dear. You see Sir, my husband and I so seldom play that—I'm afraid we haven't got one.

Prince No card room?

Mrs Wilson No. Oh, dear.

There is a pause. He is displeased, and all are aware of it

Prince Where do your guests play then?

Mrs Wilson Well ... you see sir ... they ... er well, I'm sure we can play somewhere ...

Stanley (*coming to her rescue*) What about this room, Mother? (*Pointing to the well of the stage*) In here, sir.

Prince (*glancing down*) Yes, yes. That will do very well. Where's the card table?

Mrs Wilson (*stunned again*) Card table. Yes. Well, you see, sir——

Stanley There are some spare tables here. We could put them together.

Prince (*impatiently*) Good. Good. General Williams will show you how I like things done. Where are my counters?

General Williams I'll get them Sir. Levett, give a hand with the tables.

Levett Sir.

General Williams exits

Levett is a young subaltern in the Scots Guards. He is rich and pleasant, but when the crisis hits him, he is totally out of his depth. He and Stanley clear ornaments off the tables upstage

Prince Now, who is going to play? (*He turns to Mrs Williams*) Mrs Williams?

Mrs Williams (*startled*) Oh! Well ... yes of course, sir. I don't know much about the game, but if someone will tell me what to do——

Prince It's perfectly easy——

He takes her aside to explain. Mrs Wilson crosses urgently to her son

Mrs Wilson What are we going to do?

Stanley We'll have to play.

Act I 11

Mrs Wilson But it's illegal!
Stanley It must be all right if the Prince is playing.
Mrs Wilson I suppose so ...
Levett (*having cleared one of the tables*) Where does this go?
Stanley (*at the other table*) With this one. We'll put them end to end like we do at my sister's.

General Williams returns with the baccarat cards and counters

General Williams You play do you, Mrs Green?
Ethel A little, General.
Stanley Sir William taught her.
General Williams Then she'll be an expert.
Mrs Wilson Where is Sir William, by the way?
General Williams (*looking round*) I have no idea.
Mrs Gibbs (*to Sir William*) Where were you?
Sir William Upstairs.

Sir William exits

The Prince is impatiently watching Stanley and Levett placing the two tables together

Prince That won't be long enough, you know.
Stanley There's another table over there. Help me, will you, Levett.

Levett and Stanley hurry out

The Prince is now showing increasing signs of exasperation

Prince Good heavens, we shan't start until midnight at this rate.
Mrs Wilson Oh dear. He's drumming his fingers. Lady Brooke told me that was a dangerous sign.
General Williams Mrs Green, perhaps the Prince would like a little night air?
Ethel Would you care for a turn in the garden sir, while they finish setting up the table?
Prince Very well ...
Ethel It's such a lovely evening.

Ethel and the Prince exit to the garden

As soon as Ethel has manoeuvred the Prince out, the preparations suddenly go into high gear, with frantic activity

Stanley and Levett enter with the third table

The General takes urgent charge

General Williams Hurry you two! We had better put that one in the middle. Now, we shall need a cloth and nine chairs——
Stanley Albert, George!

Mrs Williams agitatedly buttonholes Mrs Wilson

12   The Royal Baccarat Scandal

Mrs Williams Mrs Wilson, you must help me. The Prince wants me to play but I don't know a thing about it. I'm simply dreadful at cards! What am I going to do?
Mrs Wilson It's no use asking me——
General Williams (*setting up chairs*) It's quite simple, dear. I will tell you as we go along.
Mrs Williams I am bound to do everything wrong!
Stanley I'll get the cloth——

Stanley hurries out

Mrs Williams Do you know how to play, Mrs Wilson?
Mrs Wilson A little.
Mrs Williams I know I shall get muddled and trump the Prince's whatdya-callit——
General Williams That's bridge, dear. It's *baccarat* tonight.
Mrs Williams (*dazed*) It's what?
General Williams I've told you innumerable times it is perfectly simple. Don't fuss. I will look after you.

Stanley returns with a brightly coloured cloth

Stanley Will this do, sir?
General Williams It's a little highly coloured, but it'll have to. Spread it as evenly as possible—no creases.

Stanley and Levett spread the cloth over the three tables, and place ashtrays while the General puts out cards and counters

Mrs Williams What are those red things?
General Williams Counters.
Mrs Williams What are they for?
General Williams We use them instead of money. The red represents five pounds, the brown ten pounds and so on——

The Prince comes in from the centre balcony

Prince Are we all ready?
General Williams Just about, sir.
Prince Well, shall we get started then? Mrs Green will be joining us in a moment. She felt the cold and went to fetch a wrap.

They all gather round the card table

Now then, I shall be bank.
Mrs Williams I'm not quite sure what I have to do——
Prince It's perfectly easy—I am the banker—I deal two cards to the player on my right, two cards to the player on my left, and two cards to myself—the object, you understand, dear lady, is to make up the number nine.
Mrs Williams The number nine?
General Williams Or as near as possible. Eight is almost as good—say a five and a three. The player with the nearest to nine wins.

Act I

13

The Lights go down on the card players and up on the left balcony

Ethel enters quickly followed by Sir William

Ethel You are not to follow me.
Sir William Why not?
Ethel It's too dangerous.
Sir William That's half the fun.
Ethel My husband may see us.
Sir William I don't care.
Ethel It was risky enough at Blenheim, it's sheer lunacy here.
Sir William Blenheim was superb.
Ethel It was terrifying ... Suppose someone had seen us?
Sir William That's what was so exciting, don't you think?
Ethel No. No, I don't.

Sir William laughs

Be quiet. Someone will hear.
Sir William Nonsense, they are all too busy at cards.

He takes hold of her

Ethel No! You're not to! Not here.
Sir William In the conservatory then.

He kisses her. She resists at first and then succumbs

The Lights fade on them and goes up on the card players

Mrs Williams What happens if I get a ten, or one of those kings and things.
Prince Court cards don't count.
Mrs Williams Don't count!
Prince No, you see, they are more than nine, so they don't count.
Mrs Williams Not at all?
Prince No. No. Not at all. Not at any time. Kings and things, my dear lady, are useless.

Laughter

The Lights fade on the card players and goes up on the left balcony

Ethel (*breaking away*) Please ... Please stop! Why are you so reckless? It frightens me to death.
Sir William There's no fun in anything if there's no danger.
Ethel If we're caught I am the one who will suffer, not you.
Sir William We won't be caught.
Ethel You've no idea how jealous my husband can be. If he saw us alone for a moment, he'd make a dreadful scene.
Sir William He won't dare with the Prince here.
Ethel William, you must wait. We can meet in London.
Sir William We can indeed. But now we're meeting here. Your husband went to bed early, didn't he? Well you must stay up late.
Ethel I can't. He'll notice. He's a very light sleeper.

14 The Royal Baccarat Scandal

Sir William You can.

Ethel Oh God, what am I going to do? If I come to bed late there'll be another scene. What excuse can I give?

Sir William Cards.

Ethel Cards?

Sir William The Prince insisted on you staying until the end of the game.

Ethel Yes, but ...

Sir William Straight afterwards you will meet me out here again. I'll make sure the coast is clear and we will go to my room.

Ethel You must be mad——

They kiss. She breaks off suddenly

Ssh. I heard something.

Ethel is terrified and stands stock still. Sir William moves easily towards the noise

   Lycett Green steps out of the shadows

Sir William (*smiling, charmingly*) Ah, Mr Green. I was just congratulating your wife on her delightful singing.

Lycett Green Really?

Sir William It touched me to the heart, dear fellow.

   Sir William exits

Lycett Green What are you doing here?

Ethel Doing? Nothing?

Lycett Green I find that rather hard to believe.

Ethel I took the Prince out for some fresh air. I was with him until a moment ago. He went back in but I felt faint, so I stayed out here.

Lycett Green You never feel faint. In all the years I've known you you've never once fainted. I think you stayed out here to meet Gordon Cumming.

Ethel How can you say that! I did nothing of the kind. I—I— (*She suddenly bursts into tears*) Oh, it's too awful.

Lycett Green What is?

Ethel I'm so ashamed.

Lycett Green About what?

Ethel That dreadful man. He pursued me. He followed me here.

Lycett Green What happened? Tell me what happened?

Ethel He kept saying the most dreadful things to me ... He took hold of me ... I wasn't strong enough to push him away ... He tried ... to ... to kiss me. (*She sobs bitterly*)

Lycett Green is very angry but icy calm

Lycett Green No wonder you are distressed.

Ethel I thought you'd be so angry.

Lycett Green Has this ever happened before?

Ethel (*agitated*) Yes—no—Once at Blenheim he—pursued me along a

Act I   15

corridor. When I refused to talk to him he said, "You silly little fool, all the young wives go to bed with me in the end".

Lycett Green He said that?

Ethel That's why I didn't want to come this weekend. When I heard he was going to be here I was frantic.

Lycett Green I see ...

Ethel Take me home. Please take me home! I can't bear to stay here a moment longer. I can't stand the sight of him.

Lycett Green Listen to me and stop crying. We are not going.

Ethel But ...

Lycett Green We will behave as if nothing has happened. This weekend is too important to me. I'm not going to have it ruined by some disgusting old lecher.

Ethel I can't face him again!

Lycett Green Don't worry, I won't leave you alone with him for a moment. Now dry your eyes, pull yourself together, and go back to the game.

Ethel No, please.

Lycett Green (*steely hard*) The Prince will be impatient. You know he doesn't like to be kept waiting.

Pause

Ethel Very well.

Lycett Green Hurry.

She braces herself and descends the stairs. As the Lights come up in the card room, the Prince sees her

Prince Ah. Mrs Green, are you joining us at last?

Ethel I'm sorry, sir.

Prince I hope you, at least, know how to play?

Ethel I've had a few lessons.

Prince Well, I suppose that's something to be thankful for. Now—are we ever going to start? And where is Gordon Cumming hiding himself?

Sir William comes in

Sir William Here I am, sir.

Prince Thank God! At least there are two of us who know something about the game.

Sir William (*easily*) Well then, sir, we'll have the advantage, won't we?

Mrs Williams I assure you, sir, we'll all pick it up as fast as we can.

Sir William draws up his chair to the card table. He has his back to the audience, thus we cannot *see what he is doing. All the others are more or less facing him so they can see what he is doing and the audience can see their reactions to his actions*

But I'm still not quite sure what happens if I get a court card?

Sir William They don't count, Mrs Williams.

Prince I've told her that, several times.

General Williams I've spent my life telling her that.

16 The Royal Baccarat Scandal

There's a general laugh and chatter

During this, Lycett Green appears down right. No one notices this entrance on stage but the audience must. He stays in the shadows and is watching his wife and Sir William

Sir William You must get the number nine.
General Williams If you get say, two or three, you can ask for another card.
Prince To try and make nine, you see?
Mrs Williams (*clearly not seeing*) Yes. Yes, I see.
Sir William What is the bank worth, sir?
Prince Let's say a hundred, shall we?
Mrs Williams What does that mean?
General Williams It means the bank's liability is limited to a hundred pounds.
Mrs Williams Oh, is it?
Prince The bank deals. (*He does so*)
Sir William Have you any writing paper, Wilson?
Stanley I'm sure we have, sir.
Sir William Could I have a sheet, please? Preferably white.
Stanley Of course.

Stanley exits

Mrs Williams Is that part of the game?
Sir William It's difficult to see the stakes on this cloth.
Mrs Williams Stakes?
General Williams The bets. The counters, dear.
Mrs Wilson Is there something wrong with the cloth?
Sir William It's the mixture of colours. They confuse the eye.
Mrs Wilson I could get another if you like.
Prince No! No, or we'll never start.

Stanley returns quickly with a sheet of white writing paper

Stanley Here you are, sir.
Sir William I shall place my counters on this paper so that my bets are clear.

The game starts. They laugh and chat and smoke and drink

Mrs Gibbs observes and talks to the audience

Mrs Gibbs My father explained to me that there were only two real experts at the game that night.
Prince Bank deals.
Mrs Gibbs The Prince, who was preoccupied with the bank, and my father, who played with his usual dash and swagger.
Ethel We stand.
Mrs Gibbs Most bets were small——

General Williams shows his cards and laughs

—and there was great excitement when someone won a game.

Act I 17

Sir William My coup, I think.
Mrs Gibbs A coup was the term for a game. My father scrupulously placed his bets on the paper he'd asked for. His stakes were rather higher than the others.

Laughter

There was a greal deal of chatter and laughter. The gentlemen were smoking cigars and drinking brandy and port. Those not actually holding cards were watching and betting
Prince The bank gives.
Mrs Gibbs And then it happened.
Stanley My God!
Levett What's that?

Stanley pulls Levett away from the table

Stanley This is too hot.
Levett What is?
Stanley Gordon Cumming is cheating.
Ethel We draw.
Levett Impossible.
Stanley Well, see for yourself.

There's a burst of laughter from the table

Sir William Nine here!
Prince So it is.

The Prince hands Sir William his winnings and deals again. Stanley and Levett watch closely

Damn you, sir, you are having all the luck.
Mrs Williams I wish I understood why he's won.
Prince My dear lady. Don't you see Sir William has nine?
Mrs Williams Nine what?
Prince The value of his cards comes to nine, madam. Nine. The bank has to pay him the equivalent of his stake. (*Handing over the money*) Ten pounds I think, Sir William.
Sir William Five more to come, sir.

We cannot see what Sir William is doing but Stanley and Levett can and they are horrified

Stanley There! Did you see that?
Levett Yes. Yes, I did. Well, I think I did.
Stanley You think you did?
Levett I can't be sure.

There's another burst of laughter from the card table. Under cover of their laughter Stanley and Levett cross down R. Lycett Green is still there in the shadows. They do not see him

Stanley What are we to do?

18   The Royal Baccarat Scandal

Levett For goodness' sake don't ask me! I mean he's a brother officer. He's in my regiment. It's unthinkable—Gordon Cumming cheating.

Lycett Green (*stepping forward*) What's that?

Levett Oh, Lycett Green!

Lycett Green What did you say?

Levett Nothing. Nothing at all.

Lycett Green I heard you say something about Gordon Cumming?

Stanley He's juggling his counters to win more than he should.

Levett We don't know that.

Stanley (*furiously*) We do know that. We saw it. I won't stand for it. I am going to challenge him here and now.

Lycett Green (*sharply*) No.

Stanley No?

Lycett Green Not yet.

Stanley But he's robbing my mother's guests.

Lycett Green I'm sure he is. But you can't challenge him until you are certain.

Stanley I am certain.

Lycett Green Levett is not.

Stanley Levett you *know* what you saw.

Lycett Green Be quiet Stanley. Just think for a moment.

He draws Stanley away from Levett and talks urgently and quietly

If you rush up and denounce him now, what will happen? There will be a scene. Sir William will protest his innocence and Levett won't dare to support you. It'll be your word against Sir William's. A boy of twenty-two against a distinguished soldier. He'll make mincemeat of you. But if all three of us watch him—(*He moves back to Levett and now includes him in the plan*) and all three of us see him, then we will be certain and then we can accuse him.

Levett I can't do that.

Stanley Why not?

Levett I tell you, he's in my regiment.

Lycett Green Well?

Levett It will destroy him. Crucify him!

Lycett Green (*motionless*) You're quite right. It will.

Laughter

Levett, you realize it is your duty. Are you with us?

Levett (*after a moment*) Very well.

Lycett Green Then let us go back to the table.

As they do so, the game comes to an end

Prince (*rising*) Well that's settled all that for tonight. I don't know about anyone else but I'm all in—and somewhat the poorer!

Laughter

Act I 19

You had an amazing run of luck, Gordon Cumming. How do you do it? (*He beams at Sir William*)

Sir William I keep my head, sir.

Prince (*laughing*) Ha. Ha. Yes hang on to that at all costs. You always were a lucky bounder. (*He smiles at everyone graciously*) Goodnight! Goodnight! Ah, Green. You weren't playing.

Lycett Green I was delayed, sir.

Mrs Wilson (*fluttering nervously*) Let me show you to your room, sir. This is the first time you've honoured us with a visit so you may not remember the way.

Prince Thank you, dear lady. So kind.

A flurry of Parlour-maids has appeared, hovering in the background with candles

Delightful house. Delightful evening. Charming daughter. You're a lucky fellow Green.

Lycett Green Thank you, sir.

Prince (*gallantly kissing Ethel's hand*) Goodnight, my dear.

She drops a deep curtsy

Mrs Wilson There's champagne and cold chicken on a tray in your room, sir. Just in case you get hungry.

Prince (*going*) Splendid. Splendid. Lead on! Gordon Cumming.

Sir William Sir.

Prince We'll see if your luck holds out tomorrow. Goodnight.

Mrs Williams leads the Prince out, followed by all except Lycett Green, Stanley and Levett

Stanley What are we to do?

Lycett Green Watch tomorrow night.

Levett Do we have to?

Stanley Of course we have to.

Lycett Green And your mother, Stanley, must be told.

Levett Why involve Mrs Wilson?

Lycett Green She must know what is going on in her own house.

Stanley Surely if anyone is to be told, it should be my father.

Lycett Green I think not. He's far too preoccupied with this merger with the Cunard Line. It's a matter of over two million pounds.

Stanley (*whistles*) As much as that?

Lycett Green He plans to settle half a million on you and Ethel. We don't want to endanger any of that do we?

Stanley No, we don't.

Lycett Green Far better to keep him out of it for the moment.

Mrs Wilson enters

Mrs Wilson Oh, what a relief! That went off wonderfully in the end, didn't it? I think the Prince really enjoyed himself. He actually thanked me twice! Stanley help me put away these counters.

20 The Royal Baccarat Scandal

Mrs Wilson moves to the table, but Stanley doesn't follow

Stanley? Did you hear what I said? Why are you looking so solemn?

Lycett Green We have something very serious to tell you, Mrs Wilson.

Mrs Wilson Serious. Is something wrong?

Lycett Green It's about Gordon Cumming.

Mrs Wilson Oh dear. Is he ill?

Lycett Green No, nothing like that. Levett and Stanley saw him cheating at cards tonight.

Mrs Wilson What? What did you say? (*She sits*)

Stanley I know it's awful, Mother, but he was definitely cheating.

Mrs Wilson But that's impossible. He's a gentleman.

Lycett Green I'm afraid it's true.

Mrs Wilson Oh my goodness. (*She instantly starts to panic*) What are we to do? Who did you say saw him?

Lycett Green Mr Levett and Stanley.

Mrs Wilson (*staring at them*) But—but what do they know about it? They are boys. Boys! They must be mistaken. Sir William is a guards officer. A baronet. That's what he is. A baronet! They must be wrong.

Lycett Green Mrs Wilson, one of them is your own son. I'm sure you don't think he'd make such an accusation lightly.

Mrs Wilson (*rounding on her son*) Do you realize what you are saying?

Stanley I'm afraid I do, Mother.

Mrs Wilson But this is terrible. Shocking. We simply can't have a scandal. (*She bursts into tears*)

Levett Please don't distress yourself, Mrs Wilson. I am not at all certain that I saw anything.

Mrs Wilson I will not have any unpleasantness in my house. Not at any time! But especially not now with the Prince of Wales upstairs at this very moment in bed. (*She leaps up from her chair and walks about talking agitatedly*) The disgrace—it will be catastrophic. We are on the verge of an abyss or whatever it is. It'll be like the Mordunt affair or that Churchill business which was hushed up. . . . The Marlboroughs have been exiled to Ireland. That's why he's Viceroy!

Stanley Now Mother, keep calm.

Mrs Wilson Well this must be hushed up too! You're not to say a word to anyone, do you hear? I am your mother and I absolutely forbid it! It's quite simple. I will prevent anyone playing cards tomorrow. I'll tell them your father disapproves.

Lycett Green But forgive me, Mrs Wilson, that is outrageous.

Mrs Wilson Outrageous?

Lycett Green (*with quiet intensity*) This man Gordon Cumming is robbing innocent people.

Mrs Wilson Robbing them! Oh my goodness. I don't know what to do.

Lycett Green Well, I do. At all costs you must allow the game tomorrow, so we can watch it. Stanley, we shall need a different cloth. Plain coloured this time. Levett, could you fetch a piece of chalk. There's some in the billiard room.

Act I   21

Levett exits

Stanley gets a green baize cloth from the cupboard drawer

Mrs Wilson Couldn't we simply ask him to leave?
Lycett Green On what grounds? You can't do that without telling him why,
and if you accuse him without any proof he could sue you for slander.
Have you thought of that?
Mrs Wilson No! No, I haven't.

Levett returns with the chalk

*Stanley clears the table, placing glasses, ashtrays etc, the sheet of paper and
the coloured cloth on the cupboard. He covers the table with the green cloth*

Lycett Green And if he leaves without an explanation there will be every
sort of rumour going about the country in days. (*He pauses for a moment*)
Mrs Wilson, this is not the sort of thing I enjoy discussing with ladies, and
I don't know whether you realize this or not but Sir William's reputation
is not beyond reproach.
Mrs Wilson What?
Lycett Green I understand that he has a particular penchant for young
wives.
Mrs Wilson Oh my goodness. You mean ...? Do you mean people will
think he has made advances to Ethel?
Lycett Green That is exactly what everyone will think—and neither of us
wants to have that sort of gossip going the rounds, do we?
Mrs Wilson No. Oh dear me, no.
Lycett Green Then it is agreed. We will watch. We will be certain of our
facts and then we will expose him.

*He joins Levett and Stanley at the table, which is now covered with the new
cloth*

Baccarat tables usually have a line drawn round them—like this. (*He
draws a chalk line round the tablecloth about six inches from the edge of the
table*) This will make it easier for us to see if he cheats. (*He demonstrates*)
The thing to watch for is how Sir William moves his counters. (*He drops
the counter on the table and faces them*) Tomorrow evening we must all be
round the table early.
Mrs Wilson We mustn't tell anyone else.
Lycett Green Except Ethel.
Mrs Wilson Why Ethel? Must we involve——
Lycett Green She will be playing, so she must be on the look-out too. I will
make sure of it. (*He pauses*) Now I suggest we get some rest. We shall need
all our wits about us tomorrow. Not one of us must betray the slightest
hint of this at the races or over dinner. Remember, above all, that
tomorrow night at the game we have to behave as normally as possible.
No one must suspect a thing.

The stage darkens as they all exit

22   The Royal Baccarat Scandal

Mrs Gibbs is standing alone on one side

Mrs Gibbs So the trap was laid for my father.

The Lights build on the baccarat table accentuating and isolating it

We hear Ethel singing off stage—a plaintive, haunting melody

Sir William stands on the opposite side to Mrs Gibbs. He speaks over the singing

Sir William It had been a perfect day. A great crowd at the St Leger. The Prince's filly won the Clumber Stakes and I'd never seen him in a better mood. At dinner we joked, laughed, teased the ladies and swore he'd win at cards too that night. The 'baccarat' table was waiting ... They'd changed the cloth and I wondered why ... People began to wander in ...

Mrs Wilson, the Greens, Stanley and Levett enter. They come on to the central platform, then move down and stand awkwardly round the table, waiting for the Prince

The first arrivals seemed a little on edge—but I put this down to their inexperience at the game and their anxiety to acquit themselves well before the Prince. I smiled at them reassuringly. They smiled back. (*He calls out to Mrs Wilson*) A superb dinner, Mrs Wilson. Your chef excelled himself tonight.

Mrs Wilson Thank you, Sir William.

Sir William Ethel could not meet my eyes—but this, too, I thought I understood. Lycett Green was the only one who stared at me with an unflinching, steely gaze. I took no hint from it of the impending danger—only wondered with a momentary thrill whether he suspected anything about his wife. It adds to the excitement when the husband suspects.

The Prince enters with General and Mrs Williams. He is very cheerful and crosses to the card table

Prince Now, has everyone got their wits about them? I have told you, I'm in a winning mood! Ah! This is a better cloth. One can see the counters far more clearly. Sit down, sit down, please. I'll be banker again, shall I?

All Certainly, sir.

He takes his position as before

Prince Same limit as last night?
All Yes, sir.
Prince One hundred pounds?
All Yes, sir.

Ethel moves towards Sir William

Lycett Green Ethel!
Ethel I can't go through with it.
Lycett Green You have no choice.
Prince (*calling from the table*) Mrs Green. Are you playing?
Ethel I ... er ...

Act I 23

Lycett Green Of course, sir.
Ethel Yes. Yes, of course.

Ethel and Lycett Green take their places. All are now seated except Sir William, who paces the stage some distance below the table while the players prepare for the game

Mrs Gibbs cannot contain herself

Mrs Gibbs It was a monstrous plot!
Sir William (*turning to her*) Quite.
Mrs Gibbs No one warned you? Not even Mrs Green?
Sir William She couldn't.

There is a burst of conversation from the card table. Sir William slowly turns towards it then goes back to it

I was in blissful ignorance. I keenly looked forward to the game.

Sir William is again with his back to the audience and the conspirators facing him and us. Exactly as they all sit, there is simultaneously a sharp stylized cut off of sound and light, so there is now dead silence. In this silence, the entire table is suddenly silhouetted with bright back light from behind. All the figures are dark. The only direct light is on Sir William's hands. The game now commences in dumb show—slowed down perceptibly so that all the movements are quite deliberate

After a pause Mrs Gibbs speaks

Mrs Gibbs My father's hands moved. Five pairs of eyes watched. The counters clicked. A chair shifted now and then. A glass clinked and the cards fell silently onto the soft cloth.

The game continues

Mrs Williams (*who has no idea of anything*) Oh, isn't this exciting?
General Williams Great fun. I told you it would be when you got the hang of it.
Mrs Gibbs The coup was completed. The winning cards shown. The banker paid the bets. Then, to the conspirators' fascinated horror, my father seemed to walk into the trap.
Sir William There's another tenner, sir, to come here.
Prince I wish you'd put your counters so that they can be seen better. Give him another tenner, General.

The action freezes. Blackout. Pin-spots isolate the faces of the Five Witnesses staring at Sir William's hands. Each witness now speaks a short whispered thought without movement

Stanley I saw it.
Mrs Wilson How terrible.
Ethel I can't be mistaken.
Levett Just as Lycett Green said.
Lycett Green He did it.

24   The Royal Baccarat Scandal

The lights come full up and everything returns to normal. The Prince gets up from the table briskly. Having observed nothing suspicious at all, and having no idea of the drama around, he is still as cheerful and as charming as ever

Prince Another excellent game! Even though I'm poorer still. I do enjoy playing with you, Gordon Cumming. How long have we known each other?
Sir William Over twenty years, sir.
Prince Well let me tell you, you are one of my most valued friends.

The Prince crosses to Sir William, who is also in an excellent mood

Come and join me for a stroll, eh? We can talk over old times.
Sir William That would be delightful, sir.

The Prince warmly puts an arm round Sir William's shoulders and starts to lead him upstage

The Five Witnesses are standing rigid and expressionless, hardly daring to move. The Prince passes among them on his way out with Sir William

Prince Why don't you join us in the garden, Mrs Wilson?
Mrs Wilson (*hardly able to speak*) It's—it's a little chilly, sir.
Prince Yes, of course, we can't have you catching cold. Come on then, old warrior.

Beaming happily, arm round Sir William, the Prince exits, followed by the Williamses. Mrs Gibbs exits too

The Five Witnesses are left. They look at each other in silence for a moment

Lycett Green Well there's no doubt, is there?
Stanley None at all.
Mrs Wilson What on earth are we going to do?
Lycett Green There's only one thing we can do. We must inform General Williams. He is the Prince's ADC and the senior officer present.
Stanley Yes. That seems right. Who will tell him?
Lycett Green I will.
Mrs Wilson No. No. I think we should stop this here and now.
Levett I agree with Mrs Wilson. I don't want any part of it.
Lycett Green You will have to. You are a witness.
Levett Witness?
Mrs Wilson What do you mean, witness?
Lycett Green We have witnessed a crime and we must testify to that.
Mrs Wilson Oh my God ...
Lycett Green Now Levett, I want you and Stanley to join the Prince and Sir William.
Levett Join them. Why?
Lycett Green To make sure they don't come back in here.
Levett But how can we stop them?
Lycett Green Oh for God's sake man, talk!
Levett What about?

Act I   25

Lycett Green Anything, the weather, the races, your Great Aunt Maud.
Levett I haven't got an Aunt Maud.
Lycett Green Well, say anything that comes into your head. Stanley will help you. Go on—just keep them spellbound with your wit.

Lycett Green pushes Levett and Stanley out

In the meantime, Mrs Wilson, will you tell the General that I wish to see him urgently. Don't worry! We won't do anything at all without his advice.
Mrs Wilson Well if you say so. Oh I do hope you know what you are doing . . .

Mrs Wilson exits

Ethel and Lycett Green are alone

Lycett Green Ethel, I think you should go to our room.

Ethel has been a silent observer of the scene. She now speaks slowly and carefully

Ethel Are you absolutely certain you know what you are doing?
Lycett Green Absolutely.
Ethel I think you should be very careful. A scandal once started is difficult to stop. It could hurt us all.
Lycett Green The man is a cheat. I do not propose to let him get away with it. He is also a professional seducer of innocent young women. Yourself included.

Ethel stares at him in horror

You must think me a complete fool. I know exactly what has been going on for the past year. (*He speaks almost soothingly to his wife*) Oh don't look so frightened, my dear. Nothing can come out. Nothing at all. He cannot say he seduced you without destroying his own reputation as well as yours. So you see, whatever you did at Blenheim—or indeed elsewhere—he will have to be silent. You, on the other hand, will have to speak out with the rest of us about his foul play tonight. I hope you understand me?

He smiles at his wife pleasantly. She is too frightened to speak

And I saw exactly what you were up to when you tried to warn him before the game. It'll take more than that to prevent me denouncing your lover as the thief he is.

General Williams enters from the conservatory

General Williams Mrs Wilson said you wished to see me urgently.
Lycett Green Yes, sir, I do. If you will excuse us, my dear.
General Williams Well?

Ethel, without a word, without looking at her husband, turns and leaves

26   The Royal Baccarat Scandal

Lycett Green I have something most serious and unpleasant to tell you, sir. This evening, five people are convinced they saw Sir William Gordon Cumming cheat at cards.

General Williams stares at Lycett Green, appalled

General Williams Who are they?

Lycett Green Mrs Wilson and her son, Levett, my wife and myself.

General Williams All five of you saw him?

Lycett Green Yes. And all five of us cannot be wrong.

General Williams No, indeed not. You say Levett saw it too?

Lycett Green Indeed.

General Williams He is a brother officer! I mean, he would never accuse him unless he was certain.

Lycett Green Never. You must agree, sir, the man is a scoundrel, an utter——

General Williams Yes. Yes. But we must be calm. We must think what to do.

Lycett Green I am perfectly calm, sir. And I know exactly what to do. It is my intention to denounce Gordon Cumming publicly tomorrow.

General Williams (*stares at him*) You will do what?

Lycett Green I shall insult him at the race course with the whole county watching.

The General goes urgently to Lycett Green. He speaks quietly, fighting to control his anger and intense concern

General Williams Now listen to me young man. I said listen. You will in no circumstances do anything of the kind. Don't you know what's at stake here? Have you forgotten who is staying in this house? Whatever ghastly mess results from this, at all costs he must be kept out of it.

Lycett Green But why should he be involved? I am not accusing His Royal Highness of anything. I am protecting him—from a thief.

General Williams (*intensely*) Can't you understand? The Prince has been involved in an illegal game. Not only permitting it, but actually playing it. And gambling, too. You do realize that a great mass of the people regard that as a sin? What do you think the press will make of that? And the country? And, good God, the Queen? She's appalled enough at his escapades already. This might be the final straw. She might even seek to alter the succession.

Lycett Green Surely you are exaggerating, General——

General Williams The Queen is over seventy. The Prince may succeed to the throne within a matter of months—perhaps even weeks. What do you think would happen if at that very moment he was deep in a scandal?

Lycett Green But we cannot allow Gordon Cumming to get away with it. At the very least His Royal Highness must be told.

The Prince appears in the background

Prince What must I be told?

Act I   27

General Williams (*under his breath*) Damn! You are not to say anything, Green. (*Aloud*) Are you alone, sir?

The General hurries to the Prince, who is coming down the steps to the well of the stage

Prince What an extraordinary question.
General Williams Where's Gordon Cumming?
Prince He's gone to bed. Why?
General Williams Where's everyone else, sir?
Prince What on earth is the matter with you?
Lycett Green The General is upset, sir.
General Williams (*hissing*) Be quiet.
Lycett Green So is my mother-in-law. Because you see, sir——
General Williams I warn you, young-man——
Lycett Green (*carrying on deliberately*) Gordon Cumming has been seen cheating at cards.

Pause

General Williams If this gets out, sir, it will do you untold harm.
Prince Do you think I don't know that?
General Williams And to your report to the Government on Germany.
Prince Naturally. They'll throw it in the dustbin. Who saw him cheating?
General Williams I hate to tell you, sir. No less than five people.
Prince Five? This is shocking. Can they be certain? Gordon Cumming is an officer and a gentleman. I've known him twenty years.
Lycett Green We are as certain as we can be, sir.
Prince You must appreciate my position, Green. (*Gravely*) Neither the Queen nor the Government understands about Germany. But I do. I've just come back from there and I saw it all for myself. Guns. Thousands of them. A massive and sinister rearmament ... We need allies. We need France. I have to convince the powers that be. It is difficult enough as it is, but with this ... (*He picks up a handful of baccarat counters and lets them fall through his fingers*) It will be impossible. Tell me what happened. (*He stares at the card table*)
Mrs Gibbs Lycett Green was eager to give the Prince every detail. But he was speaking without authority from the other witnesses and grossly exaggerated their stories. And the Prince believed him! In his panic he never thought of demanding an immediate apology from the Wilsons for insulting his friend and their guest—he just accepted Lycett Green's story without question. And he compounded this folly by relying on General Williams for advice.
General Williams We could ask him to sign a paper undertaking not to play cards again.
Prince But wouldn't that amount to a confession?
General Williams Not necessarily. It would have to be carefully worded, of course.
Prince Why should he sign anything?
General Williams He might, if we undertook to keep silent in return.

28   The Royal Baccarat Scandal

Lycett Green jumps up excitedly

Lycett Green But that would be letting him off scot free!

General Williams It is our one hope.

Lycett Green I cannot possibly agree. If that is how you see it I shall have to take matters into my own hands. Tomorrow, at the races, I shall walk straight up to him and strike him across the face.

Prince You will do no such thing. I absolutely forbid it.

Lycett Green Sir.

Prince He must be stopped. And I assure you he will be. But not that way, and certainly not in public. Is that clear?

Lycett Green Yes, sir.

Prince Does he know about your suspicions?

Lycett Green No, sir.

Prince Then, he must be told immediately. Williams, go at once and inform him. He cannot be condemned unheard.

General Williams (*going*) Sir!

Prince (*going*) Lycett Green, have the tables cleared.

Lycett Green Sir! May I suggest that Sir William——

Prince (*sharply*) He must be allowed to defend himself!

The Prince exits

As he goes the baccarat music (heard on page 8) comes up loudly. The Lights fade down. Footmen appear and clear the stage at top speed

In a pool of light at one side Jarvis, Sir William's batman, is seen pouring a glass of brandy

Jarvis Your brandy's ready, Sir William.

Sir William enters, pulling on a dressing-gown

Sir William Thank you Jarvis. How's the back tonight?

Jarvis A little better, thank you, sir. Will you be requiring anything else?

Sir William (*stretching contentedly*) No ... I have absolutely everything I want.

Jarvis Did you have a good game, sir?

Sir William Never better, old chap. Winning streak.

Jarvis (*chuckling*) I don't know how you do it, sir.

Sir William Skill. And nerves of iron. (*He flicks a coin at him*) Here's a sovereign for you. Your share of the pickings.

Jarvis That's very generous of you, sir.

There is a knock at the door, off

Sir William See who that is will you? And you can get to bed.

Jarvis (*on his way out*) Certainly, sir. Goodnight, Sir William.

Jarvis exits

Sir William drains his brandy with immense satisfaction

General Williams enters

Act I 29

Jarvis (*off*) Good evening, General.

General Williams May I speak to you, please?

Sir William Well, I was just turning in, but if it's important . . . help yourself to a brandy.

General Williams I fear me it is most important.

Sir William Well?

General Williams Something very disagreeable has happened. Some of the people here object to the way you play baccarat.

Sir William What do you mean?

General Williams I mean they accuse you of cheating.

Sir William Of cheating?

General Williams That is correct.

Sir William stares at him as if he had suffered a physical blow. Then he rises in utter indignation

Sir William This is a foul and abominable falsehood. I never heard a more vile and unfounded accusation in my life. How dare anyone say such a thing against me? I absolutely refute these charges! I demand an explanation at once.

General Williams This is what they demand too.

Sir William I have not accused them. They accuse me. They have no right to demand anything. Whereas I insist here and now on a complete withdrawal of the charges and an instant apology. (*He is almost incoherent with rage. Shouting*) I demand an apology at once! Do you hear?

General Williams You won't get one.

Sir William What?

General Williams And I don't think they'll withdraw.

Sir William Do you understand what you are saying?

General Williams Perfectly.

Sir William They must be mad. Whoever they are, they must be stark staring mad. Who are they? I demand to know who are my accusers.

General Williams Your hostess and her son. Mr Levett. Also the Lycett Greens.

Sir William stands motionless

Sir William Both of them?

General Williams Oh yes. Both of them. Lycett Green wants to confront you at the race course tomorrow.

Sir William (*bitterly*) Two women and three boys totally without experience of life. Surely you are not going to believe the statements of these *children* against me?

General Williams One or two I could discount. But there are five, sir. Five.

Sir William You listen to me. I am a man of property, I have ample means. You can examine my bank accounts—talk to my solicitor—I am a rich man. And I will shortly be married to an American millionairess. What possible reason would I have to risk my entire reputation for a few pounds? I am an officer in the most respected regiment in the country. I belong to the best clubs. I have shot, hunted, played cards with every well-

30   The Royal Baccarat Scandal

known gentleman in the British Isles—starting with His Royal Highness—and never once has there been the slightest imputation on my honour. It is inconceivable that such a charge should be brought against me and that you, my old friend of thirty years standing, should listen to it.

General Williams I had to.

Sir William Why?

General Williams There are five of them. Are you suggesting that they are lying?

Sir William They are mistaken.

General Williams Are they all blind, sir? Are they all in a plot against you, sir? Are they all five of them motivated by malice? And if so, for what reason? Take Mrs Wilson. Why on earth should she lie about you?

Sir William I don't know.

General Williams Why should her son? Or Levett? He is in your own regiment. Surely he is a man of honour?

Sir William Of course.

General Williams Or the Lycett Greens? Have they any reason to hate you?

Sir William None whatever.

General Williams Have you hurt or damaged them in anyway?

Sir William Certainly not.

General Williams Is there a conceivable reason for any one of them to conspire against you?

Sir William None.

General Williams Well then?

Sir William If they are innocent of malice because they have no motive, I am innocent of cheating, because I, too, have no motive.

General Williams Bill, you like to win.

Sir William Well of course I do. But not that way. You know me. You know I'd never stoop to that. Apart from anything else, it's just bloody stupid.

General Williams If one person had made the accusation alone, or two even, I'd never have believed them. But five people say they saw you. Five.

Mrs Gibbs is watching from the balcony

Sir William If there were five million they'd still be mistaken. (*He turns away, to grapple with his feelings*)

Mrs Gibbs Five! They all repeated the number as if it was some magic formula for truth. No one seemed to consider examining each of the five separately to assess the value of their separate allegations.

General Williams There is, however, one point on which we can agree. This must not get out. Not just for your sake, but for His Royal Highness's sake too.

Sir William You are my old friend, my old comrade-in-arms. We've served together. Faced death together. . . . Tell me what to do.

General Williams There's little you can do yourself. But the Prince and I can help you.

Sir William (*shocked*) The Prince! He knows about this already?

General Williams I'm afraid so.

Act I 31

Sir William How could you possibly tell him before hearing my side?
General Williams Lycett Green blurted it out before I could stop him.
Sir William Lycett Green. I see. Then, I should like to see the Prince at once, if I may.
General Williams Yes, I'll see if I can arrange it.
Sir William I beg you. I need your help, Owen. I will do whatever you think best. I will place myself entirely in your hands.

As they bow formally to each other the lights go down on them but remain on Mrs Gibbs

Mrs Gibbs That was most unwise of my father. But it was not his only mistake. In fact, as I listened to him I realized he had made almost every conceivable blunder a man in his position could make. The accusation so devastated him that he was unable to defend himself sensibly. My father would come to regret each of his mistakes bitterly in time, but the most foolish of all was to tell a deliberate lie. (*She moves down to C*)

We hear a brief echo of Sir William and the General's last conversation

General Williams (*sound only*) Have the Lycett Greens any reason to hate you?
Sir William (*sound only*) None whatever.
General Williams (*sound only*) Have you hurt or damaged them in anyway?
Sir William (*sound only*) Certainly not.
Mrs Gibbs He little realized that with those words he had cut off a future lifeline. He had also gone to the core of the case—his lechery. All the young husbands hated him for preying on their wives. So he had a time-bomb ticking away under him all his life. Sooner or later one of the husbands was going to fight back—and Mr Lycett Green did.

Mrs Gibbs exits quickly

The Prince enters from the centre balcony and stands on the top step

The Lights now come up on the main stage. The Prince is facing the Five Witnesses, who have just joined him. The ladies are settling into chairs. He turns the full battery of his charm on them

Prince Do sit down. I have asked you all to come and see me again, because the General and I believe we have found a solution to this unfortunate business. We earnestly hope it will commend itself to all parties, and will prevent the matter from having wider repercussions we would all regret.

The Witnesses are all ears

I put it to you that if Gordon Cumming will sign a solemn undertaking never to play cards again, we in turn will agree never to say a word about this to anyone. What do you say?

There is a moment's pause while they digest the idea

Mrs Wilson Well, yes! I could agree to that.
Ethel I certainly could.

32   The Royal Baccarat Scandal

Levett And I.
Stanley (*after a moment, reluctantly*) Very well—but only to save any
further trouble.

Lycett Green remains silent. The Prince looks at him

Prince Well, Green?
Lycett Green I am sorry. I am truly sorry—and with great respect to you,
sir—but I simply cannot tolerate this. Not possibly. This man—this
man—is a cardsharper and a cad. Are you seriously suggesting that we let
him go out into other peoples' houses to swindle—to pick the pockets of
his friends—to—to— (*He becomes incoherent*)
Prince (*observing him dispassionately*) I think in a discussion of this nature
emotion should be kept to a minimum.
Lycett Green I am not the least emotional about it. How can you possibly
suggest such a thing, sir? I have no axe to grind personally. Not at all. I
barely know the man. But all my life I have had a horror of dishonesty. It
is obscene that this man——
Prince You really must think beyond your immediate sense of outrage.
Should this become a court case his legal advisers will quite properly
attack us all. The proposed paper, in binding us to silence, also silences
him. It protects us from any suit for slander. It also protects us from the
radical press, who will jump at the opportunity to turn this perfectly
innocent gathering into a den of illegal gambling and debauchery. None
of us will emerge unscathed. All of us will face catastrophe and that, sir,
includes the ladies. Now, do you understand?
General Williams He's right, Green. You know he is.
Mrs Wilson We simply must keep the wretched business quiet.
Stanley I think that's clear, Lycett Green.
Ethel For all our sakes, please.

Lycett Green looks at his wife for a long moment

Lycett Green Very well, I agree.
Prince Excellent. We can now draft the document. (*To the others*) Mr
Lycett Green seems to be your spokesman. Are you content for him to act
for you?
All Witnesses (*a chorus of agreement*) Yes, certainly.
Prince Very well. Perhaps the rest of you would leave us for the moment?

All exit, except the General, the Prince and Lycett Green

Lycett Green It must be strongly worded, sir.
Prince Of course. Write this down, Williams.

General Williams takes the paper Sir William used for his counters and writes

"In consideration of the promise made by the ladies and gentlemen ..."
General Williams Don't you think the ladies should be kept out of it, sir?
Prince Of course. You are quite right. "In consideration of the promise
made by the gentlemen, whose names are subscribed, to preserve silence
with reference to an accusation ..."

Act I 33

General Williams "Reference to an accusation . . ."
Prince "Which has been made in regard to my conduct at baccarat on the night of—" give the date, year and place——
Lycett Green Don't you think it should be disgraceful conduct?
Prince We mustn't drive him too far or he won't sign.
General Williams ". . . September, eighteen ninety at Tranby Croft . . ."
Prince "I will on my part solemnly undertake never to play cards again. Signed Gordon Cumming."
Lycett Green Never to play cards again as long as I live—I think the words as long as I live should be added.
Prince Yes. As long as I live. Add that, Williams. (*He turns to Lycett Green*) Are you content?
Lycett Green I am, sir.
Prince Very well. I will now see Sir William.

The General leaves the completed document on the table, goes to the entrance and beckons

(*To Lycett Green*) Perhaps you'd better wait outside with the others.

Lycett Green bows and exits the opposite side

General Williams (*announcing formally*) Sir William Gordon Cumming.

Sir William appears

Prince Come in, Gordon Cumming.
Sir William (*bowing*) Your Royal Highness.
Prince This is a sad business.
Sir William It is an outrage, sir.
Prince Dreadful. Simply dreadful.
Sir William Of course I deny the charge absolutely.
Prince (*surprised*) You deny it?
Sir William Certainly I do. I trust, sir, you do not attach any substance to it yourself?
Prince But how can you deny it? There are five of them. And they agree absolutely as to what they saw.
Sir William Sir, you know me.
Prince Very well.
Sir William For many years we have been—I venture to suggest—close personal friends.
Prince Absolutely.
Sir William Have you, in all that time, ever known me do anything dishonourable?
Prince Never.
Sir William Then may I ask why you give credit to these wild allegations?
Prince What am I to do? What is the General to do? Five honourable people accuse you.
Sir William But I have played cards all over the country for years, on the Continent as well, and no one has ever made such a preposterous suggestion!

34 The Royal Baccarat Scandal

Prince (*shrugging his shoulders*) Perhaps you have not been caught before.

Sir William again looks as if he has been struck

Sir William I cannot believe you could have made that remark, sir. You must know it is deeply wounding. Only three hours ago you referred warmly to our friendship. I am an officer and a gentleman. I have fought for my Queen and country. I have been awarded the highest decorations.

Prince Yes. Yes. Gordon Cumming, no one is disputing your courage. It is your integrity that is in question.

Sir William I thought the two went hand in hand, sir. Or will the next thing in question be my loyalty to my country?

Prince It is very shocking, but it is your word against theirs. That is the crux of the matter. (*He turns away*)

Sir William Then I must sue. That is all I can do. I will sue them for slander.

Prince No, no, Gordon Cumming, really. Do you think there is a court in the world that would believe in a conspiracy of lies against you?

Sir William Not a conspiracy, sir. A mistake. I'm prepared to grant a genuine mistake.

Prince That is even more ridiculous. Did all five make the same mistake? It is quite untenable.

Sir William Then what am I to do?

Prince General Williams here has had an excellent idea. We are your friends. We are both concerned to save you from the consequences of this unfortunate affair. If you do as we suggest, there will be no scandal. No disgrace. We can ensure that not a word of it will get out.

Sir William How?

Prince You simply have to sign a paper we have drafted.

Sir William Oh?

The Prince picks it up

Prince Before you read it, I must emphasize that I already have a solemn undertaking from your accusers to maintain absolute silence about this matter, providing you are willing to sign.

Sir William I see.

Prince I'm sure you appreciate the immense advantage of that?

Sir William May I read it?

Prince Of course.

The Prince hands Sir William the document. Sir William takes out a pair of glasses, fumbling with them slightly, and puts them on. He begins reading the document

(*Turning to the General*) I suggest we have our other friends back to witness the signing.

General Williams Certainly, sir.

The General goes to the other entrance and beckons

The Witnesses file in, led by Lycett Green

Act I   35

They all stand and wait for Sir William to finish reading. Eventually he looks up

Sir William I cannot sign this.
General Williams Why not?
Sir William It is an admission of guilt.
Lycett Green Yes, it is.
Prince (*aside; to Lycett Green*) Be quiet.
General Williams It is the only way to avoid a horrible scandal.
Sir William How can there be a scandal when I did nothing wrong?
Prince This document has been drafted for your benefit, Gordon Cumming. It is your only hope of avoiding public disgrace. Please think very carefully before you refuse.
Sir William There is no need to think. I utterly reject it. It is monstrous. Humiliating.
Lycett Green Look, why don't you just admit it and have done with it.
General Williams Will you be silent, sir!

Sir William goes furiously to Lycett Green

Sir William This is between us, isn't it, sir? You want to bring me down.
Lycett Green Yes, I do.
Sir William (*hard*) Why? I challenge you to tell me why.
Lycett Green (*looking Sir William straight in the eye*) Because you are a thief.
Sir William (*moving to hit him*) You young ... coward ...
General Williams (*stepping between them*) Stop this! This is no way to settle anything——
Lycett Green I'm not afraid of him.
General Williams You will hold your tongue, sir, or you will leave the room.

Sir William goes to the Prince

Sir William I appeal to you for your help, sir.
Prince I am trying to help you. That is the purpose of the document. Don't you see that?
Sir William I mean, in defending my honour.
Prince Unless you sign, your accusers will denounce you on the race course tomorrow morning.
Sir William But what do they say I've done?
Lycett Green You know that better than anybody.
Prince You are on the verge of disaster. You will be drummed out of your regiment. I am trying to save you from that.

General Williams holds out a pen

General Williams It is your only way out, Bill.
Sir William (*turning away*) No. Never.
General Williams You are lost if you don't sign.
Sir William I am lost if I do. How can I ever prove my innocence?

36   The Royal Baccarat Scandal

Prince (*showing signs of impatience*) Sir William, we are dealing with you as
   leniently as possible——
Sir William Dealing with me leniently! You speak as if I were a criminal. I
   tell you I am innocent! Signing that paper—if I sign—is a confession—no.
   No. I am confessing nothing, there is nothing to confess to. But the
   accusation alone damages me—in front of you, sir—it prevents me from
   associating with my friends——
General Williams No, no, quite the opposite. The document buries the
   incident for ever. You will be able to see your friends just as before. That
   is the point of it.
Sir William (*turning to the Prince*) Is that true, sir? Nothing will change?
   Particularly as far as you are concerned.
Prince (*put on the spot*) We would all certainly do our best to forget——
Sir William Tell me that you at any rate give me the benefit of the doubt in
   the matter, sir. You and General Williams, whom I have known for thirty
   years——
General Williams We have given you that with the document.
Sir William But in your own minds, I mean.
Lycett Green There is no doubt in my mind whatsoever.
General Williams Now look, for the last time, I warn you will you be
   quiet . . .
Sir William No, leave him be. He is beyond contempt. He can say what he
   likes, think what he likes. His opinion is nothing to me. (*He wheels on
   Lycett Green*) Do you hear me, nothing! It is these gentlemen—(*He turns
   to the Prince and the General, his voice breaking*) these gentlemen, who
   mean everything—their regard—their respect—are absolutely—a matter
   of life and death——
General Williams Then sign, sir. It is we who commend it to you. We who
   advise it. The Prince and I are certain it is in your best interests. You have
   no chance at all against five witnesses who are agreed upon the facts. The
   evidence is overwhelming. It could not be opposed. This is the only way.
   (*He proffers the pen again*)

Sir William looks at the document

Prince It's just a piece of paper.
General Williams It will be forgotten in a few days. Everything will be
   forgotten.
Sir William This even debars me from shilling rubbers of whist in the mess.
Lycett Green Yes, it does.
Prince (*to Green*) For the last time, sir! If you are too hard on him you will
   destroy us all.
General Williams In the last resort, Gordon Cumming, I urge you to
   consider the Prince. His position is critical. You and only you can protect
   him.
Sir William (*looking at the Prince*) You understand, sir, that if I sign, it will
   be entirely for your sake, to prevent Your Royal Highness from being
   involved in a common row. (*He takes the pen and goes to sit at the table*)
   That is strictly understood, is it not?

Act I   37

Prince Yes. Yes it is.
Sir William I ... I am not confessing to guilt.
General Williams No. No.
Sir William I am merely undertaking not to play cards again.
General Williams Quite.

Sir William is seated by now. The Prince and the General are on either side of him, waiting impatiently for him to sign. Still he hesitates

Sir William And total silence will be kept?
Prince Absolutely.
Sir William And it is understood that, apart from not playing cards, my position in society—and with you, sir, will be preserved.
Prince Of course.
Sir William Very well. With great reluctance and under extreme pressure, I will sign. (*He signs the paper*)
Prince We will all be absolutely silent. (*He signs*)
General Williams We will never mention this to a soul. (*He signs*)

Lycett Green signs silently, then speaks

Lycett Green I can assure you, Gordon Cumming, that your secret is absolutely safe in my hands. No one will ever know from me what an unspeakable monster you are.

Curtain

ACT II

When the CURTAIN *goes up Mrs Gibbs is alone on stage*

Mrs Gibbs It was only a matter of weeks before the secret was out. For anyone to have expected otherwise was naïve to the point of idiocy. Everything, literally everything, was wrong with the Tranby Croft plan. The very fact that my father scrupulously kept his side of the bargain excited comment. Why should a well-known gambler suddenly stop playing cards? Then to expect seven people to keep a secret was asking too much of human nature. Soon all London was gossiping about it. The Lycett Greens were doing rather more.

Mrs Gibbs exits

Lights up on main stage

Ethel Lycett Green enters from the centre balcony. She is carrying some flowers

Lycett Green (*off; calling*) Ethel! Ethel! Where are you?

He comes in quickly from the right

Ah! There you are. I have had a letter from General Williams.
Ethel Oh yes? I am looking for a vase.
Lycett Green About that scoundrel Gordon Cumming.
Ethel Oh? (*She finds a vase in the cupboard*) Ah!
Lycett Green It seems the secret is out.

Ethel puts the vase on the cupboard and starts to arrange her flowers.

Gordon Cumming has been getting anonymous letters.
Ethel Really?
Lycett Green You don't sound very interested in my news.
Ethel I'm not. (*She continues arranging the flowers seemingly paying no attention to him*)
Lycett Green (*looking at Ethel for a moment*) Well, perhaps this will intrigue you. Apparently Gordon Cumming has been seen with a mysterious young woman in the most unlikely places. Kew Gardens, Victoria Station—even Westminster Abbey. The latter I consider a most unsuitable place for an assignation, don't you? Was it his suggestion or yours?
Ethel There! (*She admires her arrangement*) That looks charming, doesn't it? He sent them you know. He is so reckless. I wondered when you were going to mention it as I'm afraid we guessed we were being followed. Your detective was rather clumsy. He would keep wearing the same

Act II   39

shabby overcoat. With a tear on the left sleeve. Once I'd noticed it, I could hardly fail to recognize him wherever I went. Is he outside now? Perhaps we should spare him the trouble and give him a list of where I'm going? Or perhaps you would like to come with me and meet William? That would spare you the trouble of writing to him again.

Lycett Green You think I wrote the anonymous letters?

Ethel Didn't you?

Lycett Green No.

Ethel You're not even as good a liar as William. William lies as he does everything, with practised skill.

Lycett Green Including cheating?

Ethel He didn't cheat. I'm quite sure of that. I'm also certain you wrote the letters. They are not in my view very subtle. But it was quite clever to have one sent from France. How does it go? "They are beginning to talk here of your sad adventure. If you come to Monte Carlo do not touch a card. Someone who pities you." How you must have enjoyed that last sentence.

Lycett Green I was tempted to have it out with him before, but some instinct told me to wait. If I'd merely exposed him as your lover, you would have been ruined forever, but he would have been secretly admired. But then he cheated and I knew at once that I had him where I wanted him. You see, he'd broken the code. The world may forgive an adulterer, it never forgives a cheat. I have got him where it hurts most—his honour. The clubs won't be talking about his sexual triumphs any more, but only about this bad sportsmanship. (*He stands close beside her*) Tell me, my darling what do you whisper about together in Westminster Abbey? His humiliation? The agony he is going through.

Ethel No.

Lycett Green He keeps that to himself, does he? I suppose he thrills you with tales of how he goes big-game hunting and then pops into the mess to rob his fellow officers? Does he give you a list of the Society whores he sleeps with?

Ethel That's why you hate him, isn't it? Not because he's a cheat, but because he's a man and you aren't. Perhaps you think hunting a pathetic little fox makes you one! He hunts tigers alone on foot. And your attitude to women is as cowardly and pathetic as his is brave and triumphant. Do you know, I actually married you for love? Yes, I did. I thought our first night would be the fulfilment of every possible delight, but I suffered agonies of pain and distress and you were totally unaware of anything. You were too interested in your own revolting satisfaction.

Lycett Green I won't listen to this.

Ethel Oh yes you will. You thought you could have me followed and intimidate me, but I'm not the little mouse you married. Far from it. These past months have turned me into a tigress, and I am learning to fight back.

Lycett Green You are to stop this.

Ethel (*continuing without a pause*) Our children were conceived in misery and pain and eventually in hatred—because I have come to hate you. I smile and pretend and tell my parents how happy I am and no one

40 The Royal Baccarat Scandal

suspects a thing, but I simply loathe you. Until that night in Blenheim I thought all men were as clumsy and as inconsiderate as you, but William, William was a relevation. He may swagger and boast outside the bedroom, but in it he is the most wonderful of lovers because, believe it or not, he is gentle and tender. All the young wives do sleep with him and I will tell you why. Because he is a better lover than all the young husbands put together.

There is a long pause. They stand staring at each other. Eventually Lycett Green speaks and when he does so his tone is polite and gentle. They might never have had this row

Lycett Green What are your plans for today?

It is some time before she can reply. When she does she is as polite

Ethel I'm lunching with Lady Carter, then having tea with Mother. We are going out to dinner with the Coventrys in the evening.
Lycett Green Oh yes, of course. The Prince will be there. It should be fun.
Ethel Yes.
Lycett Green I'd like you to wear the new diamonds I gave you.
Ethel Of course.
Lycett Green Will you be seeing Gordon Cumming today?
Ethel No.
Lycett Green But soon perhaps?
Ethel I don't know.
Lycett Green It would be wise not to see him at all. I gather from this letter that he is probably going to sue us all for slander.
Ethel I doubt if I shall see him again. As you have reminded me so charmingly, I am one amongst many. But if he were to ask me I would run away with him for ever.
Lycett Green I don't want to seem intrusive, but might you do that?
Ethel No. Because, you see, whilst I love him with all my heart and soul, he doesn't love me.
Lycett Green No, of course not. (*He smiles and continues with exquisite courtesy*) You realize that on the evidence I have, I could easily divorce you, but as I hope to go into politics that is out of the question.
Ethel Yes, I know.
Lycett Green Nor do I think our children should be made to suffer that stigma.
Ethel Quite so.
Lycett Green I have no wish to force myself upon you, so we will have separate bedrooms from now on.
Ethel Thank you.
Lycett Green In public—particularly in front of our families—we will continue to behave as a happy married couple.
Ethel Of course.
Lycett Green Should the bounder sue us, you will continue to support our case. You will continue to state that you saw him cheating—as he did— and you will not so much as hint—either in or out of court—at your improper relationship with him.

Act II

Ethel is silent

Should you do so, we will not only lose the case, which I realize doesn't worry you, but I will at once start divorce proceedings and you will never see your children again as long as you live.

Ethel I understand. (*She moves to go*)

Lycett Green That's not all. (*His voice remains as polite as ever*) Your father wasted a great deal of money on you with French governesses and a finishing school in Switzerland. But no amount of polish will ever disguise the fact that, at heart, you are a common Yorkshire slut. We'll meet in the hall at six. Dressed.

Ethel In my diamonds.

Lycett Green exits to the right

Ethel, with the vase of flowers, exits centre

Mrs Gibbs enters left

Mrs Gibbs And dressed in her diamonds she went, conscious of the fact that no one was discussing her jewels, however magnificent, but her role in the Tranby Croft affair. Although Society was seething with rumour, everyone tried to carry on as if nothing had happened. All except the Prince, that is. His conduct was inexplicable. In all his career he had never behaved with less generosity or less common sense. He didn't seem to understand that his attitude to my father was the crux of the plan. Everything depended on him behaving exactly as if nothing had happened.

Sir William enters angrily, followed by General Williams

Sir William For twenty years I have been invited to Lord Mar's annual shooting party for the Prince! This year I am not. And I have no doubt why. The Prince has struck my name off the guest list.

General Williams You have no proof of that.

Sir William (*ignoring him*) I signed that monstrous document on the strict understanding that secrecy would be kept and that my position in Society would be unchanged. Both pledges have been broken.

General Williams I can't believe that.

Sir William Old friends of mine walk away when I enter a room. And now the Prince has dropped me.

General Williams Oh, come now——

Sir William He refuses to see me. He ignores all my letters.

General Williams He is a busy man.

Sir William (*pulling a paper from his pocket*) Too busy to answer this? The last appeal of an old friend? (*He reads*) "The forfeiture of your esteem is, believe me, sir, the cruellest blow of all. The only hope I have of remaining an untarnished English gentleman in the eyes of the world is for the world to see no alteration in your love to me." I wrote that two weeks ago. I have not heard a word from him.

General Williams I see . . .

42 The Royal Baccarat Scandal

Sir William I want justice. It is only a matter of time now before the story is in the press. I shall have to take legal advice to protect my good name unless the Prince can be persuaded to change his attitude. Now will you speak to him for me?

General Williams My dear fellow, of course I will. You have kept your bargain, we must keep ours.

General Williams hurries out

Sir William leans against the balcony, head bowed in intense thought

Mrs Gibbs But the Prince was obdurate. He flatly refused to acknowledge my father. He had ruthlessly cut him out of his life. My father faced ostracism. The very thing he feared most. (*She looks at Sir William*) And so the long period of suspense was over. Six months of hoping against hope that the affair would be forgotten. My father made his decision.

Sir William turns, strongly

Sir William I had no alternative. I had to fight! I couldn't run away. I had done everything I could to protect the Prince. Now I had to protect myself. I was innocent. So I fought. ... And then the real nightmare started.

Mrs Gibbs Nightmare? What happened?

Sir William Once it was known that the Prince would have to go into the witness box, the newspapers scented blood. Every day there were promises of sensational disclosures and fresh attacks on me and on the Prince. They searched for sexual overtones, they described baccarat as if it was a new and terrible vice and in that atmosphere of mounting hysteria I couldn't find a barrister with courage enough even to see me, let alone take my case. Until, finally, Sir Edward Clarke called me to his chambers.

Sir Edward Clarke appears on the centre balcony. He is a self-made man, but strong both physically and in character

As he descends the steps to the well of the stage Mrs Gibbs withdraws to the side

Sir Edward Ah, Sir William! Good of you to come. Do sit down.

Sir William sits in his chair

Let me get straight to the point. I have read the papers sent to me by your solicitor. I have thought long and seriously about your case and it seems to me that you are plainly innocent. If so, then I have no doubt we will win. Justice must prevail.

Sir William Thank you.

Sir Edward But there is something very important you must understand. Whilst you are the plaintiff—that is, you are bringing the case and suing your opponents for slander—it is my experience in such cases that you will end up, at any rate in the eyes of the world, as the defendant.

Sir William Why?

Sir Edward Because they are pleading justification, and that means they are in fact accusing you of what they claim you did.

Act II 43

Sir William (*turning to Mrs Gibbs*) In other words I had to prove my innocence whilst my accusers did not have to prove my guilt.

Mrs Gibbs But that is shocking.

Sir William There's worse! (*He turns back to Sir Edward*)

Sir Edward What's more, they are accusing you of a crime. Cheating at cards for money is fraud, which is theft. If they had reported you to a policeman and he had arrested you for stealing, you would have been charged in a police court and this would have been a criminal case. But unfortunately it is not. It is a civil case. You can be attacked and cross-examined at will. Your accusers can use suggestion and innuendo against you. I am powerless to prevent it.

Sir William (*turning to Mrs Gibbs*) I was to be denied the rights of a common murderer.

Sir Edward Win or lose, you may still be damaged.

Sir William Can't we settle out of court?

Sir Edward I've tried. But this is a very peculiar case. Your opponents seem strangely obdurate. Every overture is rebuffed. I have conceded point after point. I've not even asked for an apology, merely an admission of error. They remain adamant. Why?

Sir William I don't know.

Sir Edward This is going to be a long, hard, expensive business. Our opponents have briefed Sir Charles Russell to conduct their case. We are facing one of the most formidable advocates in England. And we have the Prince of Wales against us. In order to win I have to know everything. The whole background. And the truth, sir. The complete truth.

Sir William I've told you the truth.

Sir Edward I want you to think very carefully. Is there any reason for any of your opponents to hate you?

Sir William No, sir.

Sir Edward You're sure?

Sir William Why should they? I barely know any of them.

Sir Edward Someone must. Perhaps there had been some trouble over gambling in the past?

Sir William How do you mean?

Sir Edward You like to win, don't you?

Sir William Who doesn't?

Sir Edward It is essential to you?

Sir William My father brought me up to it.

Sir Edward (*looking hard at him*) Sir William, have you cheated ever in your life?

Sir William Never.

Sir Edward That is the answer I expected. I'm sorry to have to ask such questions, but you would be surprised how often clients lie to their own counsel. (*He starts to go then stops and continues*) They lie about anything they think embarrassing. A youthful escapade best forgotten. A romantic entanglement that they don't want the world to know about. It's very stupid of them because what it means is that they send their counsel into court with one arm tied behind his back. But I am sure you are too old a soldier to do anything quite so stupid.

44 The Royal Baccarat Scandal

Sir Edward goes

Mrs Gibbs You didn't tell him about Mrs Lycett Green?
Sir William (*Standing*) How could I? Her husband may have been doing his level best to destroy me. I could not defend myself by destroying his wife. (*He turns away from her and falls silent, deep in thought*)
Mrs Gibbs I began remembering long forgotten events. Once, I think it was at Dinard, he had a run of bad luck at the casino and got into a terrible rage. (*To her father*) I remember my surprise as you hadn't lost much money—and Mother said that money had nothing to do with it. You were constitutionally incapable of being a loser.

Sir William remains silent

Then I remembered another time. There was a shoot at Gordonstoun—and Alec claimed he had a bigger bag than yours. You said no, you'd shot more than he had, and to prove it you showed him your game book. Had you altered it? Papa?

Pause

Sir William I'm sorry, my dear. You were saying?
Mrs Gibbs (*meaning the opposite*) It doesn't matter.
Sir William (*crossing to his chair*) I was remembering the first day of the trial. The huge queues outside the court waiting to get in ... (*He becomes lost in thought*)
Mrs Gibbs I wondered why he hadn't answered me. Was he unable to admit even now, that because of his need to win he had done exactly what he was accused of, so pretended not to hear me. Or had he been deliberately courting the danger of disgrace for the thrill of it, especially with the Prince there. I looked at him and I could see he was no longer aware of me. He was back in that court room.

In the background we hear the sound of a large and expectant crowd, buzzing with excitement

Sir William One had to push one's way through the crowd to get in. Inside the place was packed. It was suffocating in that hot weather. Half of Society were in the public gallery, dressed up in their best clothes. It was more like a theatre than a court room. Some of the audience had even brought opera glasses.

Spotlight on Sir William as he sits in his chair

The court begins to fill up with characters as he mentions them

There was great excitement as my five accusers arrived together.

The Five appear on the centre balcony and we hear jeers and mocking laughter from the crowd

When I caught sight of them, I was consumed with a violent anger. But for them, I would not be there. I was so furious that for a moment I nearly

Act II   45

lost control of myself. But I sat there like a rock. I was determined to betray no emotion whatsoever. Nor did I.

Mrs Gibbs But now, at long last, he was sharing his feelings with me.

Sir William The counsels arrived in their wigs and gowns, Sir Edward first, and then Sir Charles Russell.

They appear, and move briskly to their places

Sir Charles was to be my accuser and my scourge. Renowned for his merciless cross-examination, I was soon to discover how well he had earned his reputation. But the greatest sensation of all was when the Prince of Wales' carriage drew up outside.

We hear boos and cheers

The Prince, accompanied by General Williams, enters down left

The sounds reach a crescendo

General Williams is stony-faced. The Prince, however, is as genial as ever. He stands facing the audience and acknowledges the tumult graciously. He might be receiving an ovation

Prince (*smiling genially*) I shall never forgive Gordon Cumming for this. You realize he is not the only one on trial, I am too. Why the bounder didn't just go abroad I'll never know. If he wins, I shall be the laughing stock of the country.

General Williams He won't win, sir.

Prince I'm not so sure. You can never tell in slander cases.

The Prince gives a final, gracious wave, then turns to go upstage to the centre balcony. He walks straight past Sir William without a word, and sits slightly apart from the other witnesses

General Williams joins him

Sir William I tried to catch his eye, but he never so much as glanced at me. I had embarrassed him and so, quite simply, I had ceased to exist.

The tumult subsides

Mrs Gibbs is now down stage towards the side, where Sir William, centre, can easily see her. He frequently addresses her during the trial

So it began. I remember every moment of it, my feelings, the speeches for and against me, the witnesses coming and going. But it is disjointed in my mind. Like a nightmare it goes round and round, with people—barristers—everyone coming out of the dark to attack me. The struggle to keep control was so intense that sometimes I literally couldn't hear what was going on. And when I came to, it was to discover Sir Charles standing over me shouting questions. Sometimes even now I wake at night trembling at the ordeal. Can you understand that?

Mrs Gibbs Of course I can, Father.

Sir William And yet it was thirty years ago.

Mrs Gibbs But to you it was yesterday. It will always be yesterday.

46 The Royal Baccarat Scandal

An Usher appears and thumps the floor with his staff

Court Usher (*loudly*) Silence. Be upstanding in court.

All rise, face the audience, which is now both judge and jury, bow and sit

Sir Edwards rises, a spotlight on him

Sir Edward Gentlemen of the jury, (*he points to Sir William*) I am here to defend that soldier's honour. The issues are grave ones for him. If the accusation be upheld against him, there ends in this court that career of honour and of public service which his thousand friends hoped would be continued for many splendid years to come. He must go away, degraded from the profession to which he belongs, exiled from the companionship of those he has known as friends, and in another land, and perhaps under another name, seek some career which may dim, but cannot efface, the memory of these transactions. I hope for a very different result than that. I hope that Sir William Gordon Cumming may still wear in his country's service a sword that has never been stained but with the blood of it's foes, and that he, as he risked his life for you and yours in the times gone by, may, in his hour of peril here, find protection in your instincts of justice. (*He turns to Sir William and talks directly to him*) Sir William, when did you first learn of the shocking charges that were made against you? And what was your response?

Sir William I emphatically and indignantly denied them.

Sir Edward But you later signed an undertaking never to play cards again?

Sir William Yes. And I have never ceased to regret that I did so.

Sir Edward Why did you sign it?

Sir William Because extreme pressure was brought to bear on me.

Sir Edward What sort of pressure?

Sir William I was told again and again that there would be a terrible scandal if I did not.

Sir Edward You were threatened with a scandal?

Sir William Yes. Persistently threatened.

Sir Charles Russell, a spotlight on him, crosses quickly to the other side of Sir William

Sir Charles Sir William, you're a soldier and have stood up under fire on the battlefield.

Sir William Yes.

Sir Charles Yet you could not stand up to a scandal. Is that what you are saying?

Sir William No, it is not. It was a scandal to which the name of the Prince of Wales would be attached.

Sir Charles How?

Sir William It would not be desirable for the Prince to be involved with a game of baccarat.

Sir Charles Why not?

Sir William It's illegal.

Sir Charles And that is what would cause the scandal?

Act II   47

Sir William Yes.

Sir Charles Nothing to do with yourself?

Sir William No. Well, yes.

Sir Charles Which is it. Yes or no?

Sir William It would not be desirable that the name of the Prince should be associated with a game of baccarat with an officer who had been accused of cheating.

Sir Charles But you say you were not cheating. You say you were innocent. So where does the scandal come in?

Sir William I've answered that already.

Sir Charles You've done no such thing.

Sir William I was an officer in the guards. It was awkward for a man in my position.

Sir Charles Merely to be playing a game of baccarat? Why should the threat of such a trivial scandal loom so large in the mind of an innocent man? It would loom large in the mind of a guilty man because then he would be frightened of a worse scandal. That of being caught red-handed cheating at cards. Is that the scandal that frightened you, Sir William?

Sir William No, it is not.

Sir Charles Then why did you sign that paper?

Sir William I have explained that already.

Sir Charles Not to me, sir.

Sir William I was pressed to do so by the Prince and General Williams.

Sir Charles Do you suggest that they advised you to sign it believing you to be an innocent man?

Sir William I think that nothing could have been worse than the advice they gave me.

Sir Charles I was not asking whether the advice was good or bad. I want to know whether it occurred to you that they advised you in the belief that you were guilty?

Sir William (*strongly*) No. Certainly not.

Pause

Sir Charles Sir William, are you aware that the General made a detailed record of these events soon after they occurred, while they were fresh in his mind?

Sir William No, I was not aware of that.

Sir Charles A record that was read, and even signed, by the Prince of Wales as an accurate account in all respects?

Sir William I knew nothing of it.

Sir Charles Then I must point out to you that it contains the following passage: (*He reads*) "General Williams explained to Gordon Cumming that silence could only be maintained if he signed the undertaking. At the same time he clearly pointed out that his signature would be a distinct admission of guilt. Quite understanding, he signed the document."

Sir William (*appalled*) I take the strongest exception to that! It is utterly untrue! It was I, in objecting to signing, who said it would be tantamount to confession. They brushed me aside. They assured me that it wasn't. To suggest otherwise is a gross distortion of the facts!

Sir Charles resumes the attack

Sir Charles Sir William, when did you finally realize that the Prince and General Williams believed you guilty?

Sir William When I received a letter from them shortly afterwards.

Sir Charles How long ago did you receive that letter?

Sir William Nine months ago. It came as a great shock to me.

Sir Charles Why did you not retract your undertaking at once?

Sir William I thought it was impossible, having signed it.

Sir Charles You made no attempt to withdraw it?

Sir William No.

Sir Charles No attempt to vindicate yourself?

Sir William They had told me it was useless to deny the allegations.

Sir Charles But you are denying them now, aren't you?

Sir William Yes. Yes, I am.

Sir Charles Then why did you wait nine months to do so? What has altered the position?

Sir William I have told you.

Sir Charles No, you have not.

Sir William On reflection I saw the mistake I had made.

Sir Charles The mistake of cheating at cards?

Sir William No! Of signing the paper, Sir Charles, that was the mistake. But having been given an assurance that it would not come out, I lived for some time in a fool's paradise, hoping and believing that that would be the case.

Sir Charles So, although in the eyes of these once-valued and esteemed friends, you were a dishonoured man, you were content to remain so if secrecy were preserved?

Sir William It does not follow that I was guilty just because they thought so.

Sir Charles Pray attend to my question.

Sir William I have answered your question.

Sir Charles I assure you, you have not. Although you knew that in the eyes of these gentlemen, you were a dishonoured man, you were content to remain so?

Sir William I was not content to remain so.

Sir Charles Please attend! You did remain so, did you not? So what has altered the position?

Sir William I had no alternative.

Sir Charles Attend. Attend.

Sir William I am attending.

Sir Charles Answer the question!

Sir William I have answered the question.

Sir Charles You have not, Sir William. What has since taken place which has altered the position?

Sir William Are you asking me my reasons for taking these proceedings?

Sir Charles I am asking the question which I have put to you, and to which I have not yet had an answer. I will repeat it now. You knew that you were regarded, rightly or wrongly, by these esteemed friends as a man

Act II

49

with a blasted reputation. And you have said in effect that you were content not to take proceedings——

Sir Edward rises, and they argue over Sir William's head

Sir Edward Those were not the words of the witness. He said he was not content.

Sir Charles In effect.

Sir Edward Not at all! When my learned friend says "in effect" he means the very opposite.

Sir William (*hotly*) I have not had a moment's contentment since I signed that paper!

Sir Charles We are not concerned with your contentment, Sir William. We are concerned with the altered condition. Something caused you to change your mind. Something which roused you from your unsoldierly discontent?

Sir William (*strung*) Well, of course it did!

Sir Charles What was it?

Sir William The promise had been broken. The secret was all over town! The thing had become such public property that I feared it might be taken up by my clubs, by my regiment, and by all my friends.

There is a low murmur from the court, Sir William suddenly realizes that he has fallen into a trap

Sir Charles (*at length*) So your motive for taking these proceedings was not out of moral outrage, but to save yourself from social disgrace. Thank you, Sir William. That is the answer I expected long ago.

Sir Edward I call General Williams.

We hear an echo of the strange baccarat music and sounds. Everyone on stage is still

Sir William (*to Mrs Gibbs*) I felt certain I had lost. My friends had lied and betrayed me, and I could not understand why.

General Williams rises and moves into a pool of light. Sir William and Mrs Gibbs are both still clearly visible

Sir Edward General, your record of events has been read out in court. Do you claim it is accurate?

General Williams I do.

Sir Edward Sir Williams says it is not.

General Williams He is wrong.

Sir Edward Are you sure? You wrote two accounts. My learned friend has made great play with the first, in which you said he willingly signed an admission of guilt. The second was a letter to Sir William four months later. What did you say in that?

General Williams I don't remember exactly.

Sir Edward Well fortunately I have a copy.

The letter is handed to the General

50   The Royal Baccarat Scandal

Would you please read it out to the court? The marked passage.

General Williams (*reading*) "You are quite at liberty to say that you signed under extreme pressure and in no way made any acknowledgement that you were guilty."

Sir Edward So that completely contradicts your earlier account, doesn't it?

General Williams (*after a moment*) Yes, I suppose it does.

Sir Edward Thank you. Now, when you were told by Mr Lycett Green that Sir William had cheated, did you believe him?

General Williams I had no choice, five people had seen it.

Sir Edward Five. Oh, yes. Tell me, did you interview them all?

General Williams No.

Sir Edward Why not? Didn't you wish to check their stories?

General Williams It didn't seem necessary.

Sir Edward Not necessary? Sir William was an old friend of yours, wasn't he? (*Pause*) Well, wasn't he?

General Williams Yes.

Sir Edward Of thirty years' standing?

General Williams Yes.

Sir Edward How long had you known Mr Lycett Green?

General Williams Not ... very long.

Sir Edward He was a comparative stranger?

General Williams Yes.

Sir Edward And yet on the word of this stranger you immediately believed your old friend to be a cheat?

General Williams I tell you I had no choice.

Sir Edward Was it the behaviour of a friend to draw up a document which you now say was an admission of guilt, without even consulting Sir William?

General Williams I thought it was the only way out of his difficulty.

Sir Edward Was it the behaviour of a friend to persuade him to sign that document against his will?

General Williams It was for his sake.

Sir Edward Are you quite sure of that? Are you sure you did not cynically use your friendship to trap him into a confession that would hush the matter up?

General Williams (*indignantly*) No, I did not! I was quite certain he was guilty.

Sir Edward I don't think you were certain for one moment. I submit to you that you didn't care whether he was guilty or not. All you cared about was keeping the Wilson family quiet. So to this end, and this end only, you flung your old friend to the wolves.

With a meaningful look at the jury, Sir Edward moves out of his spotlight into the darkness

Sir William (*to his daughter*) Hope was returning. Sir Edward was breathing new life into my case.

Sir Charles has now moved into the light by the General. He turns to Sir William and triumphantly attacks him again

Act II   51

Sir Charles Sir William Gordon Cumming. When the General informed you that people had seen you cheating, precisely what were you accused of doing?

Sir William hesitates, caught off guard

Sir William I never knew the exact nature of the charge.
Sir Charles Presumably you asked?
Sir William I imagine so.
Sir Charles You imagine so?
Sir William Well, I must have done.

Sir Charles turns to the General

Sir Charles Did Sir William ask you, General?
General Williams No, he did not.
Sir William (*nervously*) I—I must have been too upset by the accusation. I don't remember.
Sir Charles Do you remember making any enquiries at all about this very grave accusation that had been made against you?
Sir William Yes, certainly. I asked who they were. He kept repeating that five persons made the charge.
Sir Charles Did you ask to be confronted with them?
Sir William No.
Sir Charles You did not wish to meet them face to face and demand to know what they claimed you did?
Sir William I don't think it occurred to me.
Sir Charles It didn't occur to you?
Sir William Not at the time.
Sir Charles Why not?
Sir William I had lost my head, Sir Charles, on that occasion. If I had not lost my head, I would not have signed that document.
Sir Charles I am not discussing the document. Were you not told that Mr Lycett Green wished to be confronted with you?

Sir William hesitates

Were you told that?
Sir William No.
Sir Charles Sir William Gordon Cumming, do you pledge your oath on that point?
Sir William I have no recollection of it.
Sir Charles Is that all you have to say?
Sir William I have no recollection . . . (*After a pause*) But I may go further, Sir Charles, and say emphatically that no such suggestion was made.

Sir Charles turns to General Williams who is still in the witness spot

Sir Charles Did Mr Lycett Green desire to be confronted with Sir William Gordon Cumming?
General Williams He did.
Sir Charles Did you inform Sir William?

52   The Royal Baccarat Scandal

General Williams I did.
Sir Charles Are you sure of that?
General Williams Quite sure. (*He retreats from the light*)

Sir Charles turns back to Sir William

Sir Charles Did you ask to be confronted with Mr Lycett Green?
Sir William No.
Sir Charles You knew that Mr Berkeley Levett, your own brother officer,
    was one of the accusers?
Sir William Yes.
Sir Charles Did you ask to be confronted with him?
Sir William I will save you the time, Sir Charles. I asked to be confronted
    with nobody.
Sir Charles Why not?
Sir William I cannot tell. It was an act of supreme folly on my part, but I
    did not do so. When a man is in the position I was, Sir Charles Russell, he
    is not responsible for his actions. I had a most horrible charge made
    against me, and I virtually lost my head on that occasion.
Sir Charles You are a solider of high rank with a gallant record in battle
    and great experience against all kinds of adversity?
Sir William Yes.
Sir Charles But you think you lost your head?
Sir William I consider I did.

Sir Charles turns to the jury (the audience)

Sir Charles Gentlemen, here was a man held to be of honour, facing a
    horrible charge. What did he do? He said he was innocent. A guilty man
    would say that. An innocent man would say that too, but he would say
    more. He would ask, "Where are my accusers? What do they say I have
    done? When and how do they say I did it? Bring them face to face with
    me. There is a terrible mistake which I can dispel."

*The Five Witnesses rise in a formidable group upstage, staring down at Sir
William*

Not Sir William! Instead, he enters into the degrading undertaking that he
will never, as long as he lives, play cards again, in exchange for their
secrecy. Is it conceivable that an innocent man would consent to bear
such an odious burden? Could any conduct have been more calculated to
build up, sustain, and support the evidence you will now hear of these five
honourable persons who have been accused of slander, than the conduct
of Sir William Gordon Cumming?

A rustle goes through the court, merging into the sinister baccarat sounds

Sir Charles addresses the Judge (the audience)

My Lord, to assist the court, I propose to introduce a representation of
the baccarat table, if Your Lordship pleases.

A small table, about four feet square, is brought on by two Court Officials

Act II   53

and placed downstage of Sir William's chair. It is covered with a green baize cloth on which are the necessary props such as chalk, counters and cards. Bright light builds onto it as it comes into position. At the same time the Five Witnesses slowly move down to the main stage. They stand in a group a little way upstage of the model, but they are not lit until they move to it

This is not intended to be an exact model. It is simply a device to demonstrate to the court with the greatest possible clarity the manipulation of the stakes. I call Mr Stanley Wilson.

Stanley Wilson comes forward from the group of witnesses

Will you step up to the table please?

He does so

I ask you to examine the cloth. Does it resemble the one used at Tranby Croft on the second night of the game?
Stanley It does.
Sir Charles Would you please draw a chalk line the same distance from the edge of Sir William's side of the table as it was on that night?

Stanley picks up a piece of chalk from the table and does so

Now, would you show the court a five-pound counter?

Stanley picks up a bright red counter. It is quite large—nearly three inches in diameter—and very plain to see

Please place it in the position where you saw Sir William place his stake.

Stanley does so

How would you describe that?
Stanley About six inches over the line.
Sir Charles Towards the centre of the table?
Stanley Yes.
Sir Charles That constitutes a stake—or bet—of five pounds because it is over the line?
Stanley It does.
Sir Charles Clear for all to see?
Stanley Precisely.
Sir Charles Now, will you tell me exactly what you saw the plaintiff do?
Stanley Well, as usual only two people, apart from the banker, were actually handling the cards—one on either side of the bank. The rest were betting on the cards dealt to the player on their side of the table. In this case, Sir William was betting on General Williams's cards. I noticed that Sir William had his hands together in front of him beside his stake.
Sir Charles Will you indicate that?

Stanley holds his hands together, thumb to thumb, leans forward and places them down on the table next to the five-pound counter. He is now directly beside Sir William above the table

What happened next?

54 The Royal Baccarat Scandal

Stanley The banker dealt. The General picked up his cards and Sir William leant over to see what he'd got—like this. I then noticed that he had something red in the palms of his hands, and I immediately knew this could be nothing less than another five-pound counter.

Sir Charles Show us, please.

Stanley turns over his hands. There, indeed, is a large red counter

Stanley The General had a winning nine. Immediately Sir William saw this, he withdrew his hands, leaving the counter beside his original stake, like this—(*he does so*) I turned away for a moment, and when I looked back I saw he had a third counter over the line—(*he shows this*) thus trebling his bet.

Sir Charles And trebling his winnings?

Stanley Undoubtedly.

Sir Charles turns away with a meaningful look at the jury and steps out of the light

Sir William (*drily*) He had been well rehearsed.

Sir Edward moves into the light by Stanley

Sir Edward Why did you not say at once "Sir William you only staked five pounds"?

Stanley There were ladies at the table.

Sir Edward Well?

Stanley Well, I should think that was sufficient reason for not doing so.

Sir Edward But you'd already told two ladies about such a thing the night before.

Stanley There were other ladies present. It is not a natural thing to have a scene over cards in front of ladies.

Sir Edward Tell me, have you had many scenes over the card table. You knew what should be done?

Stanley No. I have not.

Sir Edward No, indeed. How could you, when you were a novice at the game. You are a novice?

Stanley Possibly. But I know the difference between right and wrong.

Sir Edward Naturally. So you thought it would be wrong to embarrass the ladies?

Stanley Yes.

Sir Edward And wrong to make money by cheating.

Stanley Yes, of course.

Sir Edward And wrong to go on playing and letting your friends play with a man you suspected of fraud? (*Pause; hard*) That's what you did, didn't you? Well, didn't you?

Stanley I was much upset.

Sir Edward But not so upset that you stopped staking your money on cards Sir William was backing—you did do that, didn't you?

Stanley Do what?

Sir Edward Continue playing for an hour.

Act II   55

Stanley Yes, I did.
Sir Edward And staking your money on cards Sir William was backing.
Stanley Yes.
Sir Edward Yet you thought him a cheat. Tell me, Sir, what does that make you?

Stanley cannot answer. Silent and ashamed, he is lost in darkness

Mrs Wilson now moves into the witness spotlight

Mrs Wilson Oh, I've no doubt at all. Sir William definitely cheated. I saw him looking at the cards and when they were favourable I saw him push on a five pound counter with his finger straight before him so openly that I wondered others did not see it too.
Sir Charles Show us, please.
Mrs Wilson What? Oh— (*She sifts through a pile of counters*) Now which are the five-pound ones, red or brown? (*She peers at a counter*) Ah yes, here we are, the red. He put it down on the white paper, you see— (*She drops it on the floor*) Oh dear, I've dropped it! (*She disappears under the table*) Where is the thing . . . here . . . Ah, here it is! (*She reappears*) I'm so sorry. (*She puts it on the table and gives it a jab with her finger*) That's how he did it, you see—he pushed it over the line like that. I am perfectly sure that before the nine was declared his bet was only five pounds. (*She puts down a second counter*) And a moment later I saw another one there! (*She adds a third*) He was paid fifteen pounds. It came as a great shock to me, of course. I hadn't noticed anything of Sir William's play until I was passed a note from my son-in-law about it. I had completely put it out of my mind.
Sir William I could hardly wait for the cross-examination.

Sir Edward is beside her

Sir Edward Mrs Wilson.
Mrs Wilson Yes.
Sir Edward How long was it before you received the note from your son-in-law?
Mrs Wilson About an hour and a half.
Sir Edward And up to that time you had "put it completely out of your mind"?
Mrs Wilson Completely.
Sir Edward You had been told of the alleged cheating the night before. You had agreed to watch to see if he did it again. You had been reminded about it before you went into the cardroom. And you seriously say that you sat down and played for an hour and a half without the matter entering your head?
Sir William Mrs Wilson stared at Sir Edward in terror like a rabbit gazing at a cobra.
Sir Edward I would like an answer.
Mrs Wilson Yes. I am sure you would.
Sir Edward Well, what is it?

Mrs Wilson I was the hostess, you see.

Sir Edward Well?

Mrs Wilson I had plenty to think about.

Sir Edward Such as?

Mrs Wilson The dinner. The drinks. The placement at table. If Sir William left under a cloud, how was I to rearrange the seating? It was the first time the Prince had stayed with us, you see, and it was all going wrong. Dreadfully wrong. I mean my house party might have been destroyed. And then there was my daughter to think of.

Sir Edward Why your daughter particularly?

Mrs Wilson She's a young married woman, you see. I mean it would be dreadful if she was mixed up in some sort of scandal. It goes on all the time everyhere, we all know that, don't we? Not just in France where one expects it, doesn't one? But here too. In the best houses.

Sir William I could hardly breathe. Could she be referring to Ethel and me.

Mrs Wilson It goes on at Longleat—Castle Howard—Chatsworth—everywhere.

Sir Edward What goes on Mrs Wilson?

Mrs Wilson Gambling! Flinging money away on horses and cards. I should never have allowed it. I wouldn't have, if my husband hadn't gone to bed—I think—or did he come to bed later? Anyway I couldn't tell him. Didn't tell him. I'm not sure. I was once, but now I'm not. And she, Ethel, my daughter was at this card table—or was it another one— She's even a witness at this very trial. It's all too dreadful to think of. (*She bursts into tears and retreats*)

Sir William Poor Mrs Wilson. She had done what Sir Edward wanted.

Sir Edward is confronting Levett who has stepped forward

Sir Edward Tell us about the piece of paper.

Levett (*surprised*) I beg your pardon?

Sir Edward Sir William asked for a piece of paper, didn't he?

Levett I'm not sure. He may have done.

Sir Edward Well, did he or didn't he?

Levett Yes, I think so.

Sir Edward (*holding up a sheet*) Was it like this?

Levett I think so.

Sir Edward (*handing it to Levett*) Would you show us where he placed it?

Levett hesitates for a moment, then awkwardly leans across Sir William to put down the paper

Levett Er—somewhere there.

Sir Edward (*handing him three red counters*) And where did he place his stakes?

Levett (*blankly*) On the table, of course.

Sir Edward (*long suffering*) On or off the paper?

Levett Oh, on it I think.

Sir Edward Show us, please.

Levett drops one of the three counters on the paper

Act II

57

One counter. Was that his original stake?

Levett I don't remember. It may have been more.

He hesitantly drops the other two counters

Sir Edward But you don't remember.

Levett No, but I definitely saw his hand moving in a suspicious way. (*He waves a hand vaguely over the paper*)

Sir Edward Let's see what else you do remember. Were you smoking?

Levett I should think so. I don't know.

Sir Edward Were there ashtrays on the table?

Levett I can't remember. There may have been.

Sir Edward Was anything else on the table? Glasses?

Levett I daresay, if anyone was drinking. I don't know.

Sir Edward You don't remember if anyone was drinking or smoking. You don't remember if there were ashtrays or glasses. But you do remember Sir William's hand moving "in a suspicious way"?

Levett Oh yes.

Sir Edward When Stanley Wilson first told you there was something wrong, what was your response.

Levett I—I—I was appalled.

Sir Edward Did you believe it?

Levett No—not at first. I couldn't.

Sir Edward What made you change your mind?

Levett I—I realized he had raised his stake.

Sir Edward But you told me you couldn't remember how much he'd staked in the first place, so how could you know he'd raised it?

Levett I had been told he was cheating, you see. That's what I had been told.

Sir Edward So you believed it?

Levett Yes, what else was I to do?

Sir Edward Disbelieve it.

Levett I never thought of that.

Levett fades into the shadows

Sir William Three down. Two to go. But I didn't reckon with Ethel and her damnable husband.

Ethel has taken Levett's place. She seems very cool and assured

Ethel I shall need a pencil, please.

Sir Charles (*surprised*) A pencil?

Ethel I saw Sir William use a pencil.

Sir Charles (*producing one*) Like this?

Ethel Yes. That will do.

She takes it from him

Sir Charles Now, you had already seen him stake a red ten-pound counter, had you not?

Ethel No. The ten-pound counters are brown.

58   The Royal Baccarat Scandal

Sir Charles Forgive me.
Ethel Of course. (*She gives him a light smile*) It is rather complicated.
Sir Charles He had staked five pounds?
Ethel Yes.
Sir Charles Would you approach the table, please?

Ethel moves down to it. She is now standing next to Sir William

And would you kindly demonstrate to the court?

Ethel and Sir William's eyes meet. She hesitates only momentarily

Ethel Certainly. (*She picks up a red counter*) He had a red counter. Here.
Four inches beyond the line.

She places the counter. In doing so, her hand accidentally brushes Sir William's which is resting on the table. She picks up a second counter. She demonstrates each action carefully and with great precision

He had placed a second red counter very near the chalk line on this side—
almost touching it. (*She does so*) He held the pencil in his right hand. (*She does so*) He picked up his score sheet with his left. (*She does so*) Then he laid the paper over his right hand, so. When no one was looking, he carefully pushed the second counter over the line with the tip of his pencil. Like this. (*She does so*) My attention was distracted for a moment and when I turned back there was a third red counter over the line (*She places it*) His legitimate stake was five pounds. The banker paid him fifteen.

Sir William and Ethel's eyes meet again. She turns away and holds out her hand

Your pencil, I think, Sir Charles.
Sir William Where the others had been confused and contradictory, she had been calm, and lethally precise.

Lycett Green has taken Ethel's place

Sir Charles You have no doubt that the counters were pushed over the line after the cards were seen to be favourable?
Lycett Green I have no doubt of it. Sir William said, "There's another tenner to come here, sir." And the Prince said, "I wish you'd put your counters so that they can be seen better. Give him another tenner, General."
Sir Charles When you saw this, what did you do?
Lycett Green My first impulse was to jump up and expose him. But on second thoughts I felt it would be wrong to make a scene in the presence of His Royal Highness. So I got up from the table, went into the next room and wrote a note to Mrs Wilson.

Sir Charles beckons to a Court Official

Sir Charles This note was written on Tranby Croft notepaper, dated September the tenth eighteen-ninety, twelve-thirty a.m., and signed by yourself?

Act II

59

Lycett Green It was.

Sir Charles And who has had safe-keeping of it since?

Lycett Green Mrs Wilson gave it to General Williams that same evening.

The Court Official has arrived beside Lycett Green with the note on a silver salver

Sir Charles Is that the note?

Lycett Green It is.

Sir Charles Read it to the court please.

Lycett Green (*reading*) "It is perfectly horrible. I have distinctly seen Sir William Gordon Cumming cheating twice!"

Sir Charles That was written while the game was actually in progress? You walked straight out of the room and wrote it?

Lycett Green I did.

Sir Charles When the impression could not have been clearer in your mind?

Lycett Green Precisely. I wanted to record it there and then, so that no one could say later that I was confused or had imagined it.

The Court Official retires, as does Lycett Green

Sir Charles turns to the jury (the audience)

Sir Charles So, gentlemen, we have five persons swearing unmistakenly that they saw Sir William cheat, and telling you how they saw him cheat. We have two others—the Prince of Wales and General Owen Williams, who heard the accusations against him, and who arrived at the conclusion that he was guilty. We have, therefore, seven out of the eight characters in the story who have come to this clear conclusion of guilt. That is why the eighth—Sir William himself—signed the document which he was told would be regarded as an admission of guilt. And that is why General Williams advised him to do so.

Sir Edward jumps up

Sir Edward The reason he was advised to sign was to protect the reputation of the Prince of Wales!

Sir Charles No!

A sensation in court

The Prince rises as if to speak. The General restrains him

That won't do!

The two Counsels are either side of Sir William

Sir Edward There is a strong and subtle influence of Royalty. A personal influence. History is full of dishonourable deeds done by noble men who gave their honour as freely as they would have given their lives, to save the interests of a dynasty or to conceal the foibles of a prince.

A gasp goes round the court. The Prince looks increasingly angry

This is what was in the mind of General Williams. If he is to be excused

60   The Royal Baccarat Scandal

for persuading his old comrade to sign this document because of his devotion to the Prince, should not Gordon Cumming be given that credit too? Was there no loyalty to the Prince in the man who sacrificed himself, as his friends were willing to sacrifice him, in order to save the Prince's name?

Sir Charles No, sir, that will not do! I believe the Prince's name will survive the misfortune of being in the same room with a cheat!

Pause

Sir Edward You leave me with no option but to call His Royal Highness the Prince of Wales.

Dead silence. The Prince of Wales rises and moves into the witness spot

Your Royal Highness has known Sir William for twenty years?
Prince I have.
Sir Edward And for ten years at least, he has enjoyed Your Royal Highness's special favour?
Prince Certainly.
Sir Edward He has been a guest in your house?
Prince On several occasions.
Sir Edward And that friendship, that intimacy, remained unimpaired until the house party at Tranby Croft.
Prince It did.
Sir Edward Now, sir. At cards on the first evening did anything occur to give you the smallest suspicion as to Sir William's play?
Prince Nothing whatsoever.
Sir Edward Would the same apply to the game on the second evening.
Prince It would.
Sir Edward As banker, dealing the cards, on those two occasions, you saw nothing of the alleged malpractices of the plaintiff?
Prince No; it is not usual for a banker to see anything in dealing cards, especially when playing among friends in their house. You do not for a moment suspect anything of the sort.
Sir Edward Now sir. After the game on the second evening you were made aware of allegations of five individuals. Were they questioned by you, sir?
Prince No.
Sir Edward When you finally gave Sir William the honour of an interview did he deny the charge emphatically?
Prince He did.
Sir Edward Thank you, sir.

He bows respectfully and retires

Sir William I became at once profoundly uneasy. I could not put my finger on what was wrong. As Sir Charles cross-examined him, my sense of unease mounted.
Sir Charles (*now in the spotlight*) Your Royal Highness, I need hardly ask you. Were you greatly distressed by the occurrence at Tranby Croft?
Prince I was.

Act II
61

Sir Charles Did you desire to act leniently towards Sir William?

Prince (*emphatically*) Most certainly. I was motivated by concern for Sir William's welfare, and I believed that his undertaking not to play cards would in fact save him.

Sir Charles But you haven't met Sir William since?

Prince No, I haven't.

Sir Charles Have you intimated that you can never meet him again?

Prince (*in a low voice*) I cannot.

Sir Charles I'm afraid I didn't hear your Highness?

Prince I cannot.

Sir Charles Finally, what was your Royal Highness's opinion at the time of the charge against Sir William?

Pause

Prince What am I to say? (*He shrugs his shoulders helplessly in the French fashion*) They seemed so strongly supported, unanimously so, by those who brought them forward.

Sir Charles And your considered opinion as a Prince of the realm, well versed in matters of state, was that you should give credence to the charges?

Prince I felt no other course was open to me but to believe what I was told.

Sir Charles Thank you. Thank you, Your Royal Highness.

A murmur goes round the court

Sir Charles bows and retires

The light fades on the Prince

Sir William I was certain now I had lost.

Mrs Gibbs Why?

Sir William He should have re-examined! Every scrap of the Prince's evidence was hearsay. Why didn't Sir Edward challenge it? How could a jury be expected to do so if he didn't? He let the Prince say he believed I was guilty without any foundation whatsoever. The Prince had seen nothing. Nothing at all. I wanted to jump up and yell at the jury, "Don't believe him, he doesn't know what he's talking about. Just because he's a prince there is no need to pay more heed to him than to anyone else." But I didn't move. Not a muscle.

Sir Edward What is your occupation?

Lycett Green (*stepping again into the light*) I am a Master of Hounds.

Sir Edward Ah. Did you think that hunting four days a week qualified you to be the leading person in the accusations against Sir William?

Lycett Green I don't know that I was.

Sir Edward I think you were. Did you appoint yourself or were you selected?

Lycett Green Neither.

Sir Edward Nevertheless you emerged as the leader.

Lycett Green You say that. I don't.

Sir Edward Why did you dominate the whole proceedings?

62 The Royal Baccarat Scandal

Lycett Green I didn't. Not in my view.

Sir Edward You wanted to denounce Sir William. You wanted your mother-in-law to denounce him. You were the spokesman to the General and then to the Prince. You acted for the others in drafting the document. On every occasion, you are to be found furiously insisting on action. Why is that?

Lycett Green (*becoming excited*) I had every right to be furious. The man's behaviour was appalling. He had to be stopped. Had to be punished!

Pause. Sir Edward looks at him

Sir Edward Did you have any personal animosity towards Sir William?

Sir William (*suddenly bolt upright*) So that was it——

Lycett Green None whatever.

Mrs Gibbs What is it, Father?

Sir William He was looking for a personal motive. The nightmare exploded in my mind. Supposing he found it!

Suddenly Ethel is revealed in a pool of light on the opposite side of the stage

Ethel You see, my husband was upset on my behalf.

Sir Edward Your behalf?

Ethel Yes, Sir William was a guest in my mother's house.

Sir Edward Weren't you surprised that your husband was so emotional about a card game?

Ethel No. No, I wasn't.

Sir William Her nightmare was converging with mine. Would her husband give us away?

Two cross-examinations are now overlapping in Sir William's mind

Sir Edward You had no reason at all to dislike Sir William?

Lycett Green Of course not.

Ethel No, of course not! Why should he?

Sir Edward (*rounding on her*) Indeed, why should he? Can you tell us Mrs Green?

Ethel (*brief pause*) No. No, I can't.

Sir William Had Sir Edward guessed?

Sir Edward (*pressing Ethel*) Do you dislike Sir William?

Ethel No.

Sir Edward Oh, you like him do you?

Ethel (*after a fractional pause*) Not especially.

Sir Edward You know him well?

Ethel Fairly well.

Sir William How far was he prepared to go?

Sir Edward (*to Lycett Green*) You saw nothing of the cheating on the first evening, did you?

Lycett Green No.

Sir Edward Then why did you at once believe the worst of Sir William?

Lycett Green I was told what the man had done!

Ethel My brother told us. My brother wouldn't lie.

Act II   63

Sir Edward He could have been mistaken. And yet your husband leapt at once to the conclusion that Sir William was guilty. (*To Lycett Green*) You seemed incapable of any charity towards him. Why did you denounce him so passionately, so violently——
Ethel (*overwrought*) He didn't!
Sir William That's not true at all——
Ethel (*overlapping*) That's not true at all. You're distorting it all——
Sir William (*overlapping*) Distorting it all——
Sir Edward Not true? Did he not wish to challenge Sir William at the race course? To strike him across the face? (*He wheels on Lycett Green*) You said that, didn't you? To both the General and the Prince?
Lycett Green (*losing his temper*) What if I did? He deserved to be challenged. To be assaulted.
Ethel (*to herself*) No, please——
Sir Edward (*overlapping*) Go on——
Lycett Green His behaviour was disgraceful. Despicable——
Ethel (*to herself*) Please——
Sir William (*overlapping*) Please——
Sir Edward (*overlapping*) Yes, Mr Green?
Lycett Green Utterly scandalous!
Sir Edward Yes?
Lycett Green Why, he even——

Ethel gives a cry and sinks to the floor

Sir William Her children . . .

There is a sensation in court. Court officials run to her

Sir Edward A chair for the witness!
Sir William She was frightened of losing her children.

The Officials help Ethel to her feet

Sir Edward Are you all right, Mrs Green?
Ethel Yes, I'm all right. Thank you. I'm sorry. It must have been the heat——
Sir Edward (*drily*) The heat. Of course. Perhaps you'd like to sit down?

Ethel nods. The Officials help her to a seat

(*To Lycett Green*) My point, Mr Green, is this. Could you not have given Sir William the benefit of the doubt?
Lycett Green We did. We watched him on the second night to make sure.

The light fades on Lycett Green

Sir Edward consults his brief

Sir William He had come to a dead end. But it had been a close shave. I breathed a sigh of relief. But not for long.
Sir Edward My Lord, I would like to recall Mrs Green, when the witness is sufficiently recoverd.

64   The Royal Baccarat Scandal

Sir William Ethel looked at me. She knew as well as I did that if she let slip one hint of our relationship, she faced catastrophe. You see, we had been meeting secretly until the trial.

Mrs Gibbs Wasn't that terribly dangerous?

Sir William Oh yes. In eighteen-ninety a divorced woman was an outcast. Would she be able to face Sir Edward out?

Ethel is in the witness spot again

Sir Edward (*to Ethel*) You say you knew Sir William fairly well. Surely you know him better than that?

Ethel No. Casually.

Sir Edward You have often been a fellow-guest with him at house parties?

Ethel Oh yes.

Sir Edward Did you ever find anything unusual about his behaviour?

Ethel Unusual?

Sir Edward You never noticed him cheating at cards for example?

Ethel No.

Sir Edward At which house parties did you meet him?

Ethel Usually at his sister's, of whom I am very fond.

Sir Edward Anywhere else?

Ethel Possibly.

Sir Edward Blenheim Palace, for instance?

Sir William That was a shock to both of us.

Pause

Ethel (*cautiously*) I've stayed there only once.

Sir William Had someone seen us and talked?

Sir Edward Was Sir William a fellow-guest?

Ethel There were a great many guests. The Duke of Marlborough is most hospitable. I really can't recall if Sir William was there or not.

Sir Edward You can't recall if he was there?

Ethel No.

Sir Edward Isn't that rather odd?

Ethel I don't see why. It was a long time ago. I don't keep a diary.

Sir William She was skating on dreadfully thin ice.

Sir Edward Have you played baccarat often?

Ethel No.

Sir Edward How many times would you say?

Sir William Perhaps Blenheim was just a lucky guess.

Sir Edward Did you hear me, Mrs Green? I asked you how many times you've played baccarat.

Ethel About six or seven times.

Sir Edward Who taught you?

Ethel Sir William Gordon Cumming.

Sir Edward Did you enjoy the lessons?

Ethel Yes.

Sir Edward Did he teach you any other games?

Ethel No.

Act II   65

Sir William She was clever enough to keep her answers short.
Sir Edward When did he teach you?
Ethel About a year ago.
Sir Edward Where did he teach you?
Ethel At my house in York. He came to dinner and stayed overnight.
Sir Edward And you've only played six or seven times since?
Ethel Yes.
Sir Edward So you don't really know much about the game?
Ethel I think I do.
Sir Edward How can you, with so little experience?
Ethel Sir William is an expert teacher.
Sir Edward Ah, I see. Sir William is an expert teacher.
Ethel Yes.
Sir Edward And you are a novice?
Ethel I was.
Sir Edward But after his expert instructions you were no longer a novice?
Ethel That is my opinion.
Sir Edward A fellow-guest recalls you playing very badly at a certain house
    party.
Ethel I don't think I play badly.
Sir Edward It was at Blenheim Palace, he said.
Sir William So he did know something.
Sir Edward Did you play badly at Blenheim?
Ethel I don't recall it.
Sir Edward He said you were flushed and excited during the game.
Ethel Oh?
Sir Edward Were you flushed and excited at Blenheim Palace?
Ethel I have no recollection of being excited there at all.
Sir Edward Or at Tranby Croft? Were you excited that Sir William was a
    fellow-guest?
Ethel Not particularly.
Sir Edward What was your reaction when you were told he had cheated?
Ethel I was shocked.
Sir Edward Did you believe it?
Ethel I—I didn't know what to believe.
Sir Edward But you were upset.
Ethel Yes, dreadfully.
Sir Edward But you agreed to watch him the next night?
Ethel Yes.
Sir Edward You didn't think to warn him?
Ethel Warn him?
Sir Edward You didn't think to advise him not to play again?
Ethel No.
Sir Edward And you agreed to the setting of the trap?
Ethel I agreed to watch him with the others.
Sir Edward You didn't consider this a betrayal?
Ethel Betrayal?
Sir Edward Of an old and valued friend?

66   The Royal Baccarat Scandal

There is silence. Ethel seems to be on the verge of tears

Sir William The conflict was almost too much for her. She knew Sir Edward
was forcing her to betray me at that very moment. She could have saved
me by giving in to him. But her own survival was at stake. I longed to go
to her rescue. I wanted to leap up and shout at Sir Edward, "Leave her
alone!" I wanted to yell at the judge and the jury that we were lovers. I
wanted to go to her and say, "We'll both be outcasts together. Leave your
husband and we'll fight for your children." But I forced myself to be
silent. To the end of my days I will wonder what would have happened if I
had said what was in my heart. But for her sake I was silent.

Sir Edward Mrs Green, didn't you hear my question?

With great difficulty Ethel manages to control herself

Ethel Yes. I heard you.
Sir Edward I require an answer.
Ethel No. I did not consider it a betrayal of an old friend.
Sir Edward No further questions.

Sir Edward moves away and the light fades on Ethel

Sir William She'd come through with flying colours.
Mrs Gibbs Yes, and so had you.
Sir William I'd never admired her more.
Mrs Gibbs For the first time in his life he really cared for a woman, cared
what happened to her. Letting her betray him was the one unselfish act in
his life. (*To Sir William*) You must have loved her very much.

Sir William looks at his daughter

Sir William Yes.
Mrs Gibbs And she never knew?
Sir William No.
Mrs Gibbs You never told her?
Sir William I couldn't. Not before, because I didn't know it myself; and not
after, because it was too late. It was only then in the court room, as she
desperately stuck her knife into me, that I knew I loved her. And knew I
had lost her. And was convinced I'd lost my case. And then I could hardly
believe it. That bastard Lycett Green was really under attack at last.

*Sir Edward is hammering fast and hard at Lycett Green who is now in the
spotlight*

Sir Edward Is it the practice to say what the stakes are?
Lycett Green I do not know.
Sir Edward You do not know enough of baccarat to say if the banker
declares the stakes?
Lycett Green No.
Sir Edward Will you tell us how many people staked as much as ten pounds,
fifteen pounds or twenty pounds.

Act II   67

Lycett Green I cannot do so.

Sir Edward I suppose you thought it a very serious thing to charge a man with cheating?

Lycett Green I think so.

Sir Edward Having so little knowledge of the game yourself, would you not ask some questions?

Lycett Green As to the cheating?

Sir Edward As to what was alleged with regard to the play at the game of baccarat?

Lycett Green If you saw a man, as soon as he had seen his card, increase his stake, you must know he is cheating.

Sir Edward Even if you are entirely ignorant of the game?

Lycett Green I should think so.

Sir Edward You agree that you are entirely ignorant of the game?

Lycett Green No. I do not agree.

Sir Edward You have just demonstrated your ignorance. Why do you think the court should give any weight to your opinion?

Lycett Green I can't answer for the court.

Sir Edward Are you, in fact able to form an opinion at all?

Lycett Green I have no doubt that he was cheating. No doubt at all. I would stake my life on it.

Sir Edward Very well. (*He pauses, looks at the jury, and then speaks very deliberately*) Mr Lycett Green, have you ever heard of anybody playing baccarat according to a system?

Lycett Green (*mystified*) A system?

Sir Edward Yes, a particular method of play?

Lycett Green I cannot say.

Sir Edward Did you ever hear of a system called the "Coup de Trois"?

Lycett Green Not that I know of.

Sir Edward Really? Then perhaps Sir William can enlighten you. (*He turns to Sir William*) Sir William, like many expert players of baccarat, do you employ a system?

Sir William Yes, I do.

Sir Edward Will you tell the court what it is called?

Sir William The Coup de Trois.

Sir Edward Did you play that system at Tranby Croft?

Sir William I did.

Sir Edward Would you please explain it to the court—and to Mr Lycett Green, of course. Perhaps you could demonstrate it for us?

Sir William Certainly. I stake one five-pound counter, like this. (*He does so*) If I win, a five-pound counter comes to me from the bank and I add that to my original stake, like this. (*He does so*) Then I add a further five-pound counter of my own, like this, making three counters—worth fifteen pounds. (*He does so*) That is my stake for the next coup.

Sir Edward And that is the system you were working—the Coup de Trois, or game of three?

Sir William Indeed.

Sir Edward When you win, you leave your original stake down on the table,

68 The Royal Baccarat Scandal

add to it what you have just won, and also add a counter of the same value from your own pile?

Sir William Precisely.

Sir Edward Now, I want the jury to be quite clear about this. You would be seen, under this system, to add two identical counters to your original stake?

Sir William That is so.

Sir Edward The crucial question is when. Did you make these additions before or after the banker paid out?

Sir William After, naturally.

Sir Edward To do so before, when you knew you had won, would be cheating?

Sir William Most certainly.

Sir Edward But you did not do this?

Sir William (*firmly*) No. It was not possible. Under the system, one of the counters I added had to be my payment from the bank.

Sir Edward Now, Sir William, could you tell us in what circumstances your actions, in following this perfectly legitimate method of play, might have been misinterpreted as cheating?

Sir William If there were inexperienced players present who might not be familiar with the system.

Sir Edward looks at Lycett Green

Sir Edward Or even know of its existence?

Sir William Exactly so.

Sir Edward And were such players present?

Sir William As it now appears, yes.

The Witnesses shift uneasily. Lycett Green steps out of the light

Sir Edward Now, on the second night, when you joined the game, were you aware that no less than five persons, including your hostess, were watching to see if you cheated?

Sir William Absolutely not.

Sir Edward And did you use the same system throughout the evening?

Sir William (*very firmly*) I did.

There is a sensation, followed by shouts of "Order Order" and the judge's gavel being banged, Sir Edward turns to the jury

Sir Edward Gentlemen, that is the case for the plaintiff. The Wilson family were inexperienced players. They blundered and were mistaken and falsely attacked the character of an honourable gentleman. No experienced player saw any misconduct whatsoever. And, gentleman, just let me draw your attention to this. Nobody other than Stanley Wilson saw any foul play except a person who had been told beforehand that he was going to see it. A person, therefore, who was *expecting* to see it. Take Mrs Wilson. She saw nothing for one and a half hours, but immediately her son-in-law reminded her what they were looking for—she saw it! Under stress of emotion, Gentlemen, a suggestion all too easily becomes a

Act II   69

reality. Take Mr Levett. What did he say under cross-examination? "I had been told he had been cheating." In that remark lies the revelation of the whole thing.

Sir William I freely forgave Sir Edward's inept handling of the Prince, as he ruthlessly demolished the defendants' case.

Sir Edward Gentlemen, just consider what you are being asked to believe. A wealthy man, who has been playing cards for twenty years without provoking the least suspicion, suddenly becomes a blackguard in order to win a few pounds that he doesn't need from the Prince of Wales, upon whose goodwill and patronage his future depends. For this he puts his whole career at stake. And you will notice something else for it is very remarkable. For a man intending to deceive some of the keenest eyes in Europe Sir William is quite extraordinary. He selects a RED counter, the brightest of all. He puts it on a WHITE paper, the clearest of all. He draws attention to it by saying to the Prince, "my stakes are on the white paper". (*He shows the court*) And as you see for yourselves, it is about the most conspicuous combination that could possibly be invented! But then everyone's behaviour is extraordinary. Each of the witnesses has come before you and utterly destroyed their credibility. Take the Master of the Hounds. Mr Lycett Green is the person who said that if they found him cheating they would expose him. Quite right. It is at the card table, and nowhere else, that such a thing should be denounced. So Mr Lycett Green sees Sir William push counters across the table. Immediately the Master of Foxhounds knows what ought to be done. He knows that then and there, on the spot, at any cost, you should make an accusation, or forever hold your peace about it. So he jumps up, full of valiant resolution, and he goes away—and writes to his mother-in-law!

There is a burst of laughter. Lycett Green rises, furiously

It is ridiculous to talk of the evidence of people like this as grounds upon which a life is to be ruined and a reputation wrecked. I ask you, in his name, to clear him of this charge. It is not too late for you to prevent this gallant officer from being sacrificed to protect The Prince of Wales. The motto of his race is "Without fear". He came without fear into the witness-box, for he had nothing to conceal. He sits without fear at this moment, for he believes, as I believe, that justice is safe in the hands of a British jury.

Sir Edward moves out of the spotlight

Sir William I sat back. Radiant. Confident. It was all over bar the shouting. We had unquestionably won.

The Five Witnesses turn their backs on Sir William and exit upstage. The court empties

Mrs Gibbs But you lost.
Sir William Yes.
Mrs Gibbs But, in heaven's name, why?

Sir William Because of the Prince and the judge. The jury could not believe a man the Prince of Wales thought guilty, could possibly be innocent. So I was condemned.

Mrs Gibbs And the judge, Father, what of the judge?

Sir William Ah yes. You must go and look up all the old newspapers. Even now after all these years I cannot speak of him. Or his summing up.

Mrs Gibbs No, of course not.

He turns to go, then stops, his back is to her

Sir William I was crucified.

Mrs Gibbs Yes.

She stands quite still. He speaks almost dispassionately

Sir William His name was Lord Coleridge. He had been, I understand, a formidable advocate in his day. He was certainly an admirable advocate for the defendants. He started his summing up, gently, quietly, and I knew at once it was disaster. As he mentioned my accusers one by one he cooed indulgently. All of them were perfect. All. He saw nothing foolish, hasty or unwise in anything they did. Then he turned on my case. Baccarat. He didn't understand Coup de Trois and he didn't expect the jury to either. Sir Edward was an Officer of the Crown. Did the jury know that? They might think Sir Edward's duty was to the Prince and not to me. For Royalty is great! Then gradually his voice changed as he began on me. He sneered at all I stood for. I was a moral coward. It was ridiculous to say that I had been forced to sign. I had betrayed my friends, I had tried to hide behind the Prince of Wales. I was disloyal. By the time he had finished with me I felt like a traitor to my country.

Mrs Gibbs moves towards him. He moves away, whether by accident or design she doesn't know. He sits and continues as before in a voice devoid of emotion

It was described as the most disgraceful summing up in history. Biased and unfair. He all but instructed the jury to find against me. And so they filed out to discuss my case—an action which had lasted five whole days. And do you know how long it was before they came back? (*He pauses and looks at his daughter*) Thirteen minutes.

Mrs Gibbs (*deeply shocked*) That is outrageous.

Sir William Thirteen minutes to discuss the rules of baccarat, which probably none of them had even played. Thirteen minutes to debate every point made by both counsels. Thirteen minutes to weigh the evidence of those idiotic witnesses. Thirteen minutes to decide my fate and ... of course there was an outcry. Of course the jury was booed and hissed. Of course all the papers attacked the judge. The Queen dispensed with my services, the Archbishop of Canterbury preached a sermon against the Prince, and his report on Germany was flung in the dustbin. And then within a week, all anyone ever remembered was that I had lost. As it was a civil case I wasn't sent to prison. Instead I was confined to infinite freedom. I can go anywhere I like—but I can go nowhere. No one will receive me.

Act II

Mrs Gibbs I do not think I had ever felt so sad. All his life he had despised a large majority of the human race—and now it was the other way round. I looked at him and longed to comfort him but I didn't know how. (*To Sir William*) Did you ever see Mrs Green again?

Sir William Once. Just after the war. I went to London on business and I was in a taxi one evening in a traffic jam. A car, a Rolls Royce, drew level, and in the back was a beautiful woman. She was in evening dress wearing diamonds. It was her. I'm sure it was her. She turned and stared at me. Neither of us gave any sign, we just looked at each other. And I knew that her life had ended with mine. And then the traffic moved on—and she was gone.

A pause

Mrs Gibbs Why did you marry my mother?

Sir William For her money. And to have a son.

Mrs Gibbs Was that really all she meant to you?

Sir William Yes.

Mrs Gibbs And you never discussed the case?

Sir William Not really. After we'd been married twenty years, a newspaper wrote an article about me and the trial. Your mother read it in silence. "Is it accurate?" she said. "As far as it goes," I said. I knew she hadn't had much of a life with me, so I tried—I tried for the only time in my marriage—to tell her something of what I've just told you. When I finished, she looked at me and said, "Yes. But what I want to know is this. Did you cheat?"

Mrs Gibbs What did you say?

Sir William I said . . . I said . . . "Frankly, my dear, I've forgotten." (*He gets up to go, then he hesitates. He takes Mrs Gibbs' hand awkwardly and pats it. He smiles at her and pats it again*)

Sir William exits

CURTAIN

FURNITURE AND PROPERTY LIST

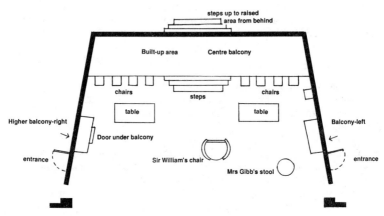

ACT I

On stage: Up stage
  Built-up area with wide steps in the centre and a pillar; steps up to built-up area from behind
  Raised balcony, left
  Higher balcony, right. *Under it:* a door
  Two tables. *On them:* ornaments, ashtrays
  Nine hard-backed chairs
  Suggestion of oak panelling, hunting trophies, regimental souvenirs
  Down stage
  Chair, large but easily movable
  Comfortable tapestry stool
  Small cupboard. *On it:* bowl of punch, punch glasses, decanter of brandy, brandy glasses, other refreshments. *Inside it:* a vase. *In a drawer:* green baize cloth

Off stage: Glass of brandy, cigar, baccarat cards and counters **(General Williams)**
  Shirt, cravat, buttonhole **(Girl in negligée)**
  Vases of flowers, linen, candles **(Parlourmaids)**
  Trays of glasses, champagne buckets **(Footmen)**
  Cigar, drinks **(House Guests)**
  Table **(Stanley and Levett)**
  Brightly coloured tablecloth, sheet of white writing paper **(Stanley)**
  Shawl **(Ethel)**
  Piece of chalk
  Drinks, cigars **(Card Players)**
  Dressing-gown **(Sir William)**

The Royal Baccarat Scandal

Personal: **General Williams:** pen, money (Victorian bank notes)
Sir William: sovereign coin in pocket, pair of glasses in pocket

ACT II

Strike: Glasses, refreshments, ashtrays, decanter of brandy and glasses, etc., from the top of the cupboard, tables

Set: Arrange chairs for courtroom

Off stage: Flowers **(Ethel)**
Small table, about four feet square, covered by green baize cloth. *On it:* baccarat counters and cards, a piece of chalk, and a piece of white writing paper **(two Court Officials)**
Silver salver. *On it:* a note **(Court Offical)**

Personal: **Sir Charles:** pencil

LIGHTING PLOT

A basic lighting plot is given here, as suggested by cues in the script. This plot can be varied according to each production's needs

To open: Light on Sir William, down stage. Up stage shadowy

Cue 1	**General Williams** appears *Light up on General Williams and two Young Men*	(Page 2)
Cue 2	**General Williams:** "My lips are sealed." *Fade light on General Williams; light up on Prince of Wales and Girl*	(Page 3)
Cue 3	**Prince of Wales:** "He's such an understanding man." *Fade light on Prince of Wales and Girl; light up on Sir William and Mrs Gibbs*	(Page 4)
Cue 3	**Sir William:** "... even the Prince of Wales." *Cross-fade to Sir William and the Prince*	(Page 4)
Cue 5	**Prince of Wales** exits *Fade light to spot on Sir William*	(Page 4)
Cue 6	**Sir William** exits *Lights up on main stage*	(Page 5)
Cue 7	**Ethel:** "You can't make me go." *Light off Ethel; spotlight on Sir William on right balcony*	(Page 8)
Cue 8	**Sir William:** "... and fraught with peril." *Light up on main stage*	(Page 8)
Cue 9	**Mrs Wilson:** "... I shall scream." *Light down on main stage. Crossfade to Sir William and Mrs Gibbs*	(Page 9)
Cue 10	**Sir William:** "... Ethel Lycett Green sang to us." *Fade spot on Sir William: lights up on main stage*	(Page 9)
Cue 11	**General Williams:** "... the nearest to nine wins." *Lights down on card players; lights up on left balcony*	(Page 12)
Cue 12	**Sir William** kisses **Ethel**. She resists and then succumbs *Fade lights on Sir William and Ethel; lights up on Card Players*	(Page 13)
Cue 13	**Prince:** "... Kings and things, my dear lady, are useless." *Fade lights on Card Players; Lights up on left balcony*	(Page 13)
Cue 14	**Ethel** comes down the stairs *Lights up on card room*	(Page 15)
Cue 15	**All** (except **Mrs Gibbs**) exit *Fade Lights except on Mrs Gibbs*	(Page 21)

The Royal Baccarat Scandal   75

Cue 16	**Mrs Gibbs:** "So the trap was laid for my father."	(Page 22)
	Build lights on baccarat table	
Cue 17	**Card players** sit	(Page 23)
	Sharp, stylized cut-off of light. Suddenly silhouette table with bright back light from behind, leaving all figures in darkness, except for direct light on Sir William's hands	
Cue 18	**Prince:** "Give him another tenner, General." Action freezes	(Page 23)
	Blackout; isolate Lycett Green, Ethel, Stanley, Mrs Wilson and Levett, and Sir William's hands, with pin spots	
Cue 19	**Lycett Green:** "He did it."	(Page 23)
	Lights up to full	
Cue 20	**Prince:** "He must be allowed to defend himself."	(Page 28)
	Fade light on main stage; pool of light on Jarvis and Sir William at one side	
Cue 21	**Sir William** and **General Williams** bow	(Page 31)
	Lights down on Sir William and General Williams. Light on Mrs Gibbs	
Cue 22	**Prince** enters	(Page 31)
	Lights up on main stage	

ACT II

To open:	Lights on Mrs Gibbs	
Cue 23	**Mrs Gibbs** exits	(Page 38)
	Cut spotlight. Bring up main lights	
Cue 24	**Ethel** exits	(Page 41)
	Light left balcony	
Cue 25	**Mrs Gibbs:** ". . . nothing had happened."	(Page 41)
	Lights up on main stage	
Cue 26	**Sir William** sits in his chair	(Page 44)
	Spotlight on Sir William	
Cue 27	**Sir Edward** rises	(Page 46)
	Spotlight on Sir Edward. Darken main stage	
Cue 28	**Sir William:** "Persistently threatened."	(Page 46)
	Spotlight on Sir Charles	
Cue 29	**General Williams** rises	(Page 49)
	Pool of light—the "witness" spot; hold light on Sir William and Mrs Gibbs	
Cue 30	Table brought in by two **Court Officials**	(Page 53)
	Build bright light on table as it is put into position; this is now the "witness" spotlight	
Cue 31	**Lycett Green, Ethel, Stanley, Mrs Wilson** and **Levett** move to stand by the table	(Page 53)
	Light on them when they have taken up their positions	
Cue 32	**Sir Charles** bows and retires	(Page 61)
	Fade light on Prince	

76 The Royal Baccarat Scandal

Cue 33	**Sir William:** ".., Supposing he found it!" *Spotlight on Ethel*	(Page 62)
Cue 34	**Lycett Green:** "... second night to make sure." *Light fades on Lycett Green*	(Page 63)
Cue 35	**Sir William:** "... to face Sir Edward out?" *Spot on Ethel*	(Page 64)
Cue 36	**Sir Edward** moves away *Light fades on Ethel*	(Page 66)
Cue 37	**Sir William:** "... under attack at last". *Lights up on Lycett Green*	(Page 66)
Cue 38	**Sir Edward** moves out of spotlight *Fade spotlight. Lights up on main stage*	(Page 69)

EFFECTS PLOT

ACT I

Cue 1	**Sir William:** "Baccarat ..." *Echo of strange music, with sound of clicking counters and distant voices murmuring the jargon of the baccarat game*	(Page 8)
Cue 2	**Sir William:** "... Ethel Lycett Green sang to us ..." *Fade in Ethel's voice singing the end of a song; applause*	(Page 9)
Cue 3	Light builds on baccarat table *Sound of Ethel singing a plaintive, haunting melody, off stage*	(Page 22)
Cue 4	**Card Players** sit *Sharp, stylized cut-off of sound*	(Page 23)
Cue 5	**Mrs Gibbs:** "My father's hands moved ... cards fell silently onto the soft cloth." *Sounds of the game: clicking counters, shifting chairs, clinking glass*	(Page 23)
Cue 6	**Prince** exits *Baccarat music to cover change. Cut when lights upon Jarvis*	(Page 28)
Cue 7	**Mrs Gibbs:** "... to tell a deliberate lie." *Echo of Sir William and the General's last conversation*	(Page 31)

ACT II

Cue 8	**Mrs Gibbs:** "He was back in that courtroom." *Background sound of a large, expectant crowd buzzing with excitement*	(Page 44)
Cue 9	**Lycett Green, Ethel, Levett, Stanley** and **Mrs Wilson** appear on the centre balcony *Jeers and mocking laughter from the crowd*	(Page 44)
Cue 10	**Sir William:** "... the Prince of Wales' carriage drew up outside." *Boos and jeers from the crowd*	(Page 45)
Cue 11	**Prince** and **General Williams** enter *Boos and jeers reach crescendo*	(Page 45)
Cue 12	**Sir William:** "... I had ceased to exist." *Crowd sounds subside*	(Page 45)
Cue 13	**Sir Charles:** "That is the answer I expected long ago." *Echo of strange baccarat music and sounds (as Cue 1)*	(Page 49)

78 The Royal Baccarat Scandal

Cue 14 **Sir Charles:** "... the conduct of Sir William Gordon Cumming?" (Page 52)
*Rustle goes through court, merging into the sinister baccarat
sounds*

Cue 15 **Sir William:** "I did." (Page 68)
*Crowd uproar, followed by shouts of "Order, order" and the
sound of a judge's gavel being banged*

Cue 16 **Sir Edward:** "—and writes to his mother-in-law!" (Page 69)
Burst of laughter

MADE AND PRINTED IN GREAT BRITAIN BY
LATIMER TREND & COMPANY LTD PLYMOUTH
MADE IN ENGLAND